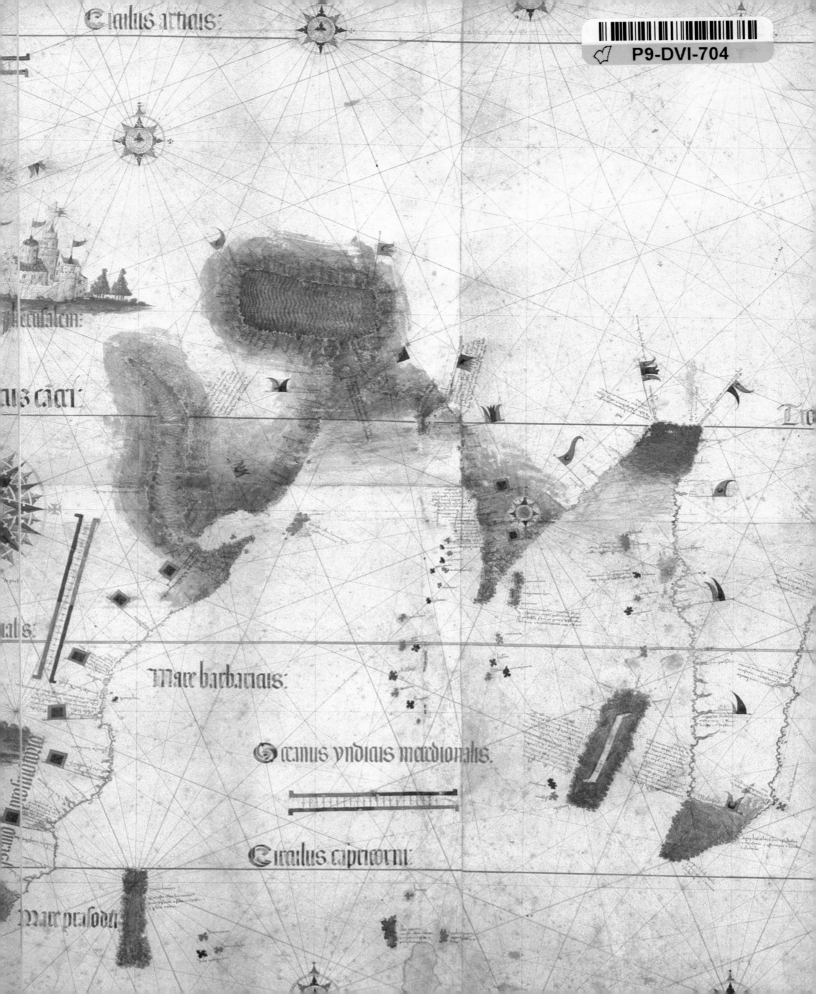

Circulus articus:

Iherusalem:

Mare barbaricus:

Oceanus yndicus meridionalis.

Circulus capricorni:

Mare prasodis

**Rand McNally**
**Children's Atlas of World History**
First published in 1988 by Kingfisher Books Ltd.
Copyright © Grisewood & Dempsey Ltd., 1988

Printed in Italy

Library of Congress Catalog Card No. 88-061951
ISBN 528-83349-9

# ⊕ Rand McNally
## Children's Atlas of
# World
# History

**Rand McNally & Company**

Chicago • New York • San Francisco

# Contents

# The World We Live In

People's lives have always been shaped by the places they live in. The food they eat, the clothes they wear, the houses they build, and the work they do all depend on their surroundings.

But people have also done a great deal to shape the places they have settled in. From early times on, they have cleared forests and drained marshes to provide good farming land. Channels have been dug to carry water to crops, and dams built to store water for the dry seasons. This has helped the land produce more food. People have also been very destructive. They have cut down forests to provide timber and churned up the land to get rock, coal, and other minerals. In recent times smoke and dirt from factories and cars, and chemicals used on the land, have poisoned the air, much of the land, rivers, and even part of the sea.

The histories of nations have been influenced very greatly by the areas in which people live and the different ways they have changed their surroundings. In this book we look at history and geography together, and see how the countries of today have developed.

One way in which people have changed the world they live in is by irrigating, or watering, the land so that they can farm it. This Egyptian is using an ox to turn a wheel raising pots of water from a large channel to a smaller one. Methods like this have been used for thousands of years.

People have polluted the Earth with industrial waste and smoke (below) and used its resources carelessly.

# THE ANCIENT WORLD

The story of the past is often divided into five periods. The first of these is ancient history. Strictly speaking, it begins when people first learned to write about 5,500 years ago. The time before that is known as prehistory. The other periods are the Middle Ages, the ages of discovery and of revolutions, and the modern age.

The first real people lived on Earth about two million years ago. We know a lot about them and about the sort of lives they lived by studying their bones, the things they made, and the pictures they painted. Once they had learned how to write things down they left a record of their lives and piecing together the story of the past became much easier.

**The Americas**
● The first people reached America (1) about 30,000 years ago across the land bridge between Asia and Alaska that existed during the Ice Ages.
● In about 3000 B.C. there were people in Central America (2) and Peru (3) where they lived by hunting and food gathering, but beans and corn were beginning to be farmed.
● By A.D. 500 the Maya of Central America had built ceremonial centers in the low-lying forests. On the coast of Peru pottery and textiles were produced.

**North Africa**
● Carthage (4) was founded by the Phoenicians in 814 B.C.
● North Africa (5) prospered under the Romans. Vines, grain, and olives were grown on irrigated land, and cities were built.

**Egypt**
● Upper and Lower Egypt (6) became one kingdom in 3100 B.C. The main gods were worshiped in elaborate temples. Gold and copper were used and *hieroglyphic* writing developed.
● In A.D. 30 Egypt became a Roman province.

**Persia**
● In the 500s B.C. the Persian Empire (7) expanded. It stretched from Egypt in the west to India in the east, but by A.D. 117 the Persians came under the rule of the Roman Empire.

**Greece**
● In the 2000s B.C. the Minoans of Crete (11) became important traders. But by the 1450s B.C. the centers of Crete were destroyed, except for Knossos, which was taken over by the Mycenaeans of Greece (12). Their empire collapsed in the 1200s B.C..
● In 776 B.C. the first Olympic Games were held in Greece.

**Bible Lands**
● In about 2000 B.C. Abraham led his tribe into the Bible Lands of Canaan (10).
● Jesus was born about 4 B.C. in Bethlehem and in A.D. 30 he was crucified by the Romans.

**Fertile Crescent**
● Farming began in the area called the "Fertile Crescent" (9) in the Near East in the 8000s B.C.

**Mesopotamia**
● In the 3000s B.C. the first cities grew up in Mesopotamia (8) and writing was developed there.
● In 539 B.C. the Persians captured Babylonia in Mesopotamia and took control of the region.

## Greece

- From 900–750 B.C. the Greek city-states emerged and the Empire spread around the Mediterranean.
- Alexander the Great became king of Macedon in 336 B.C. He soon ruled all of Greece, and conquered the Persian Empire.
- In 146 B.C. Greece came under Roman rule.

## Rome

- In 510 B.C. the Roman Republic (13) was founded.
- In 61 B.C. Julius Caesar, the Roman general, won his first major victories. He went on to rule Rome but was murdered in 44 B.C. His great nephew, Octavian, became the first emperor.

- In 116 A.D. the Roman Empire was at its greatest under the emperor, Trajan.
- The last Roman emperor in the West gave up his throne to the barbarians in A.D. 476.

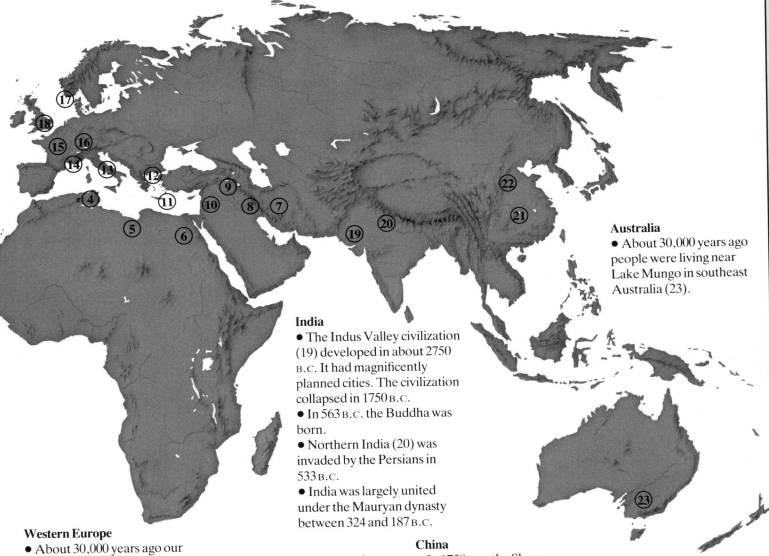

## Australia

- About 30,000 years ago people were living near Lake Mungo in southeast Australia (23).

## India

- The Indus Valley civilization (19) developed in about 2750 B.C. It had magnificently planned cities. The civilization collapsed in 1750 B.C.
- In 563 B.C. the Buddha was born.
- Northern India (20) was invaded by the Persians in 533 B.C.
- India was largely united under the Mauryan dynasty between 324 and 187 B.C.

## Western Europe

- About 30,000 years ago our ancestors lived at Cro-Magnon in southern France (14). They were the first people just like us.
- The Bronze Age was established in northern and western Europe (17) and Stonehenge was completed in Britain (18).

- From 700 B.C. the iron-using Hallstatt culture spread out from Austria (16).
- In 450 B.C. the Celtic La Tène culture developed in France (15), with its delicate metalwork and beautiful gold ornaments.

## China

- In 1750 B.C. the Shang dynasty was founded in China (21).
- Confucius was born in 551 B.C. Iron casting was developed and silk, pottery, lacquerwork, bronzes, and stone carving were produced.

- The Ch'in dynasty came to power in 221 B.C. and gave the country its name. Under it the Great Wall (22) of China was built to keep out the northern invaders.

# The First People

No one knows for certain just how people came into being. But about two million years ago some early people were living in Africa. They walked upright, as we do, and they made themselves tools of stone. But they looked very different from us. They were shorter and hairier, with heavy brows and huge jaws.

These early people found food by gathering roots, fruits, and seeds, and by hunting animals for meat. Over thousands of years they changed and became more and more like modern people. They learned how to use fire, and how to make clothes out of animal skins. At some time they began to talk. We learn about them from their bones and from the tools they left behind.

By 30,000 years ago people whose bodies were the same shape as ours were living in many parts of the world. At that time the Earth's climate was colder than it is now, and great herds of animals such as mammoths, caribou, and moose wandered over the icy plains of Europe, central Asia, and America. Some people lived in shelters made of skin and branches, or of animal bones. Others lived in caves in the rocks.

About 10,000 years ago the world grew warmer. Some of the big mammals died out, and others moved far north, where it was still cold. Over a very long period of time people gradually learned how to be farmers.

Now people no longer needed to move about in search of food. They could settle down in villages, which they built of local materials. As the animals became tamer, they could be milked and used to carry loads. Wool from the sheep was collected, and soon people learned how to spin it into thread and weave it into cloth. They made pots of clay and discovered metal to make strong tools.

There was a region of good farmland which stretched from Egypt to Mesopotamia (see pages 12–13). This region is often called the Fertile Crescent.

Above: The first people were skillful carvers. This bison is carved from an antler.

Left: A painting of a bison from the cave of Altamira in northern Spain. The Altamira paintings were first discovered in 1879. Early people mainly painted large animals which they hunted for food. Possibly they thought that by painting the animals they held some sort of magical power over them, and would have greater success in hunting. Well over a hundred decorated caves have so far been discovered in France and Spain.

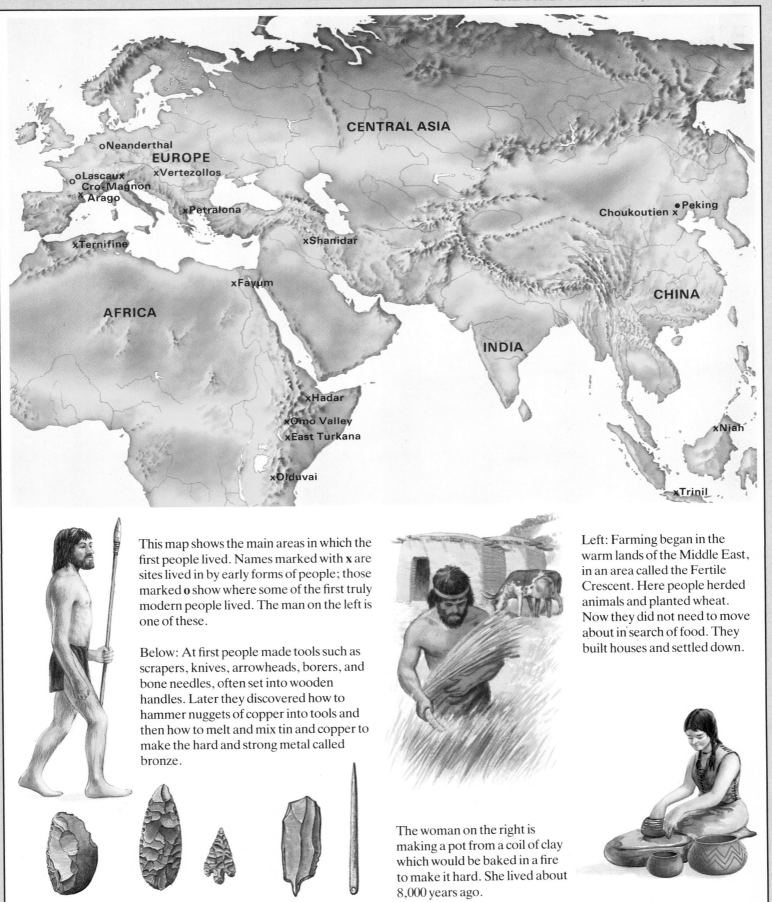

CENTRAL ASIA

oNeanderthal
EUROPE
xVertezollos
oLascaux
Cro-Magnon
o
xArago
xPetralona

Choukoutien x   •Peking

xShanidar

xTernifine

CHINA

xFayum

AFRICA

INDIA

xHadar
xOmo Valley
xEast Turkana

xNiah

xOlduvai

xTrinil

This map shows the main areas in which the first people lived. Names marked with **x** are sites lived in by early forms of people; those marked **o** show where some of the first truly modern people lived. The man on the left is one of these.

Below: At first people made tools such as scrapers, knives, arrowheads, borers, and bone needles, often set into wooden handles. Later they discovered how to hammer nuggets of copper into tools and then how to melt and mix tin and copper to make the hard and strong metal called bronze.

Left: Farming began in the warm lands of the Middle East, in an area called the Fertile Crescent. Here people herded animals and planted wheat. Now they did not need to move about in search of food. They built houses and settled down.

The woman on the right is making a pot from a coil of clay which would be baked in a fire to make it hard. She lived about 8,000 years ago.

11

# Mesopotamia

Mesopotamia means the "Land between the Two Rivers." These two rivers are the Tigris and the Euphrates. The southern part of ancient Mesopotamia is called Sumer. This is a hot, dry place that gets very little rain, but the farmers of Sumer dug networks of ditches to store the flood water from the rivers and then let it run into the fields where it was needed. The soil was good for growing crops and the Sumerians had plenty of food to spare.

They used the extra food to support craftsmen who made tools, pots, furniture, clothes, jewels, and weapons. The farmers paid the priests and they paid taxes to their kings. Food and crafts were also sold to foreigners and in return they bought stone, wood, and metal.

In this way the Sumerians grew rich, and their numbers increased. By 3200 B.C. they had started living in great cities, each with its own ruler. The houses were made of mud bricks that had been baked hard in the hot sun. The streets were narrow, but the houses of the rich were comfortable and cool.

First one, then another Sumerian city grew powerful enough to rule over the others. But about 2350 B.C. power passed from the cities of Sumer to the land of Akkad to the north. The Akkadians ruled over the first great empire. From then on the ruling power in Mesopotamia changed many times, as different cities or peoples grew stronger. About 1730 B.C. Sumer and Akkad were under the rule of the kings of Babylon. The most famous early king of Babylon was Hammurabi.

About 880 B.C. the Assyrians from the north rose to power. But the Babylonians grew strong once more. They rose in revolt against the Assyrians, and took over their empire in 612 B.C.. Less than a hundred years later, Babylon itself fell victim to the Persians from the east.

### Writing

As they grew wealthy, the Sumerians needed to make records of their goods. At first they drew objects, for example, a bull or an ear of wheat, on a clay tablet. As time passed the pictures got more and more simple, until they were just groups of wedge-shaped marks (left) that no longer made pictures. We call this writing *cuneiform*, meaning wedge-shaped.

Left: The *ziggurat* at Ur was built by the Sumerians around 2100 B.C. Ziggurats were temple towers built of mud bricks, roughly in the shape of a pyramid. They had tall platforms built one on top of the other, with a stairway right to the top, where the temple was built. Like most ancient peoples, the Sumerians believed in many gods and goddesses who ruled this world and the Next World after death. They made many offerings to keep the gods happy, and the priests held services in their honor.

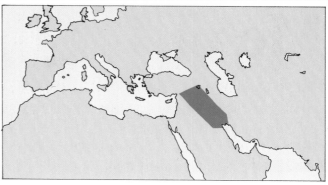

Left: Some of the early people of Sumer lived in the marshes and built huts and boats of reeds, just like ones built by the people living there today.

Below: The upper map shows the region of Mesopotamia and the lower one shows the area around it. The Assyrian Empire stretched as far west as Egypt. The picture at the top left shows people from the city of Ur in Sumer, in about 2500 B.C. Servants drive cattle, sheep and goats, and labourers carry heavy loads. At this time Sumer was a rich and important market, and traders from India and from the Mediterranean visited it. The bottom right picture shows Assyrian warriors. The Assyrians were very warlike and were greatly feared by the peoples over whom they ruled. They carved many stone slabs with scenes like this.

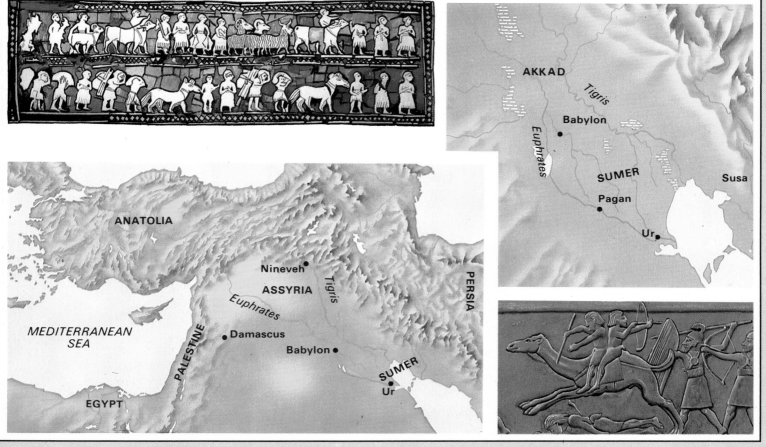

# Egypt

Egypt had once been two lands, Upper (south) and Lower (north) Egypt. The lands were united into one kingdom in about 3100 B.C., but the kings went on wearing two crowns and calling themselves king of Upper and of Lower Egypt. Kings were also believed to be the sons of Ra, the Sun god. The Egyptian king was called the *pharaoh*. This comes from two Egyptian words *per-o*, meaning Great House—that is, the palace. The Egyptians felt it was not polite to refer directly to the king, so they said the palace instead.

Dynasties (families of kings) changed and there were some very troubled times, and even invasions by foreigners, but Egypt's way of life went on with little change. Except for a few short spells, it stayed a free land from 3100 to 30 B.C., when it became part of the Roman Empire.

The Egyptians were very clever builders. As part of the taxes they owed to the king, peasants worked for him, building temples and his tomb. Some of the kings had great pyramids built of stone for their tombs.

All Egyptians believed that there was a life after death so they put food, clothing, jewels, and furniture in their tombs. The hot, dry sand of the desert where they were buried has preserved the contents of many of these tombs until the present day. This is why we know so much about how people lived in Ancient Egypt. They painted the tomb walls with scenes of daily life and we can also learn a lot from these pictures.

Above: This tomb painting shows people from Africa bringing gifts of a gold chain, fruit, and a leopard skin to the pharaoh. Gold from Nubia was the source of a great deal of Egypt's wealth. This picture dates from about 1400 B.C.

Left: This little monkey is made of glazed earthenware. Monkeys, like cats and dogs, were popular pets in Egypt.

Below: The death mask of Tutankhamun, made of solid gold inlaid with glass and semi-precious stones. Tutankhamun became pharaoh of Egypt when he was only nine years old. He died nine years later in 1352 B.C. His tomb was discovered in the Valley of the Kings at Thebes in 1922.

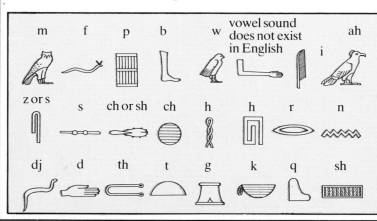

| m | f | p | b | w | vowel sound does not exist in English | ah |
| z or s | s | ch or sh | ch | h | h | r | n |
| dj | d | th | t | g | k | q | sh |

## Writing

The earliest kind of writing used in Egypt we call *hieroglyphs*. It is a script made up of picture signs. Some of these signs had the value of one letter of our alphabet, but others represented two or more.

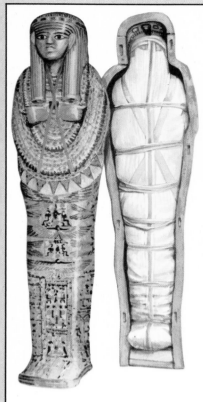

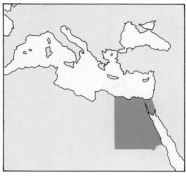

Left: The mummy and coffin of a priestess showing the elaborate wrappings. The Egyptians believed that if you were to enjoy the Next World properly, your earthly body had to survive. So they learned how to preserve bodies by using special salts and wrapping them in linen bandages. This process is called *mummification*.

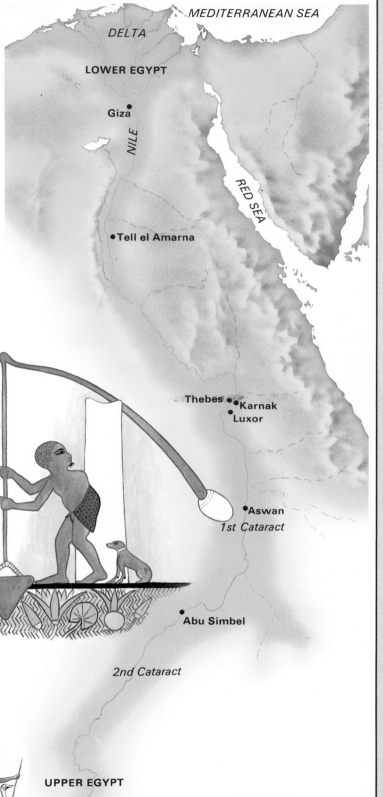

The picture on the right shows a man using a *shaduf* to raise water. The weight at the end of the curved pole balanced the water in his bucket, which he dipped in the river and then swung around to empty in a smaller channel. Farmers made canals, dykes, and little channels to carry water from the river to their fields.

Egypt stretches for about 600 miles north to south, along the banks of the river Nile. There is little or no rainfall, but every June, before the modern dams were built, the river flooded, covering the land with rich black mud. This made it very fertile. When the floods went down the farmers plowed and sowed the soil, which was so rich that they could sometimes grow two crops before the hot season began. In the background of the picture below are the three great pyramids at Giza, built as tombs for pharaohs. They were built in the desert, so that no land which could be farmed was wasted. They are more than 4,000 years old, and were one of the Seven Wonders of the Ancient World.

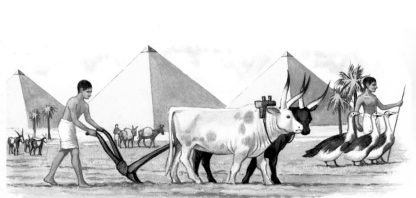

MEDITERRANEAN SEA

DELTA

LOWER EGYPT

Giza

NILE

RED SEA

Tell el Amarna

Thebes • Karnak
Luxor

Aswan
1st Cataract

Abu Simbel

2nd Cataract

UPPER EGYPT

3rd Cataract

4th Cataract    5th Cataract

NUBIA

15

# The Bible Lands

The Bible Land of Canaan runs north to south along the east coast of the Mediterranean. Today it is divided up between Israel, Jordan, Lebanon, and Syria. In ancient times Canaan lay between two powerful countries—Egypt and Mesopotamia.

The Israelites, or Jews as they later became known, were just one of many peoples living in this area. Many of them, like the Israelites, were wandering herdsmen who moved about in search of good grazing. The Bible tells us that Abraham led in a group of herdsmen (probably in about 2000 B.C.), and their descendants moved down to Egypt a few hundred years later, again in search of new grazing. When Moses led the Israelites back to Canaan they settled down west of the river Jordan and began to farm there. They defeated the people around, and set up a kingdom with its capital at Jerusalem. But to the east great empires were growing up. Assyrians and then Babylonians moved into the area. Many of the people were taken to the great city of Babylon as slaves. They stayed there until it was conquered by the Persians and they were freed. Next the Greeks under Alexander moved in, and when Jesus was born the area was under Roman rule.

Above: This painting from an Egyptian tomb, dating from about 1200 B.C., shows merchants from Syria with their goods. The trade routes from Mesopotamia and Anatolia to Egypt passed through the Bible Lands.

Below: This hillside in Israel has been terraced so that vines can be grown there. Much of Canaan was very fertile, receiving more rainfall than the deserts to the north and east. Vines have been cultivated in Canaan for thousands of years, and the Bible often mentions wine and vineyards. Crops of barley and wheat were also grown and sheep and goats grazed together with donkeys and oxen.

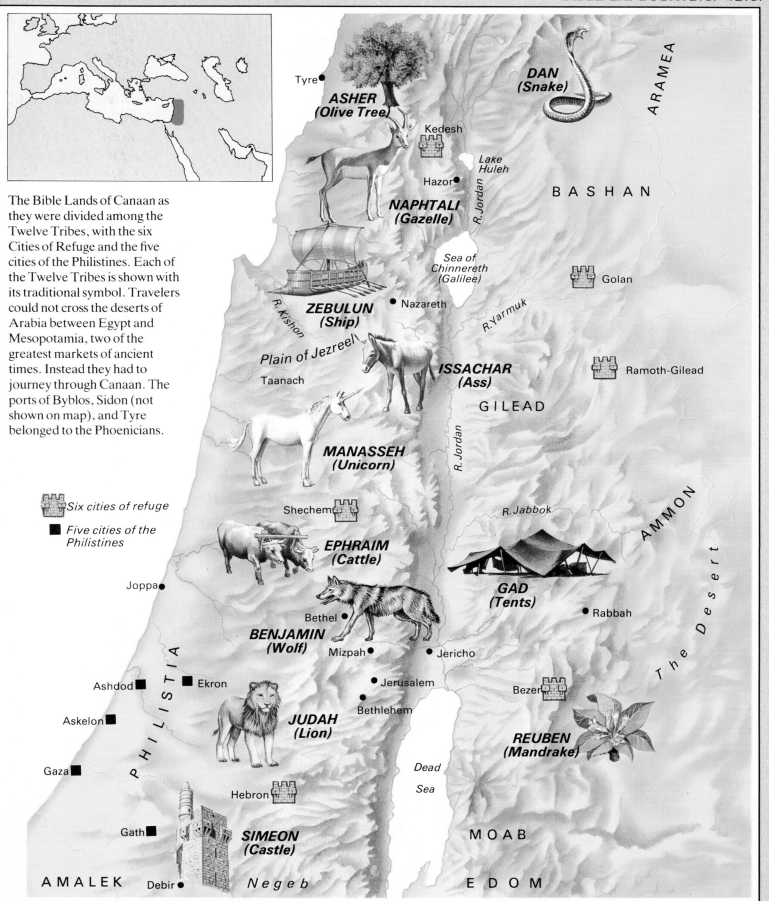

**ASHER
(Olive Tree)**

Tyre

**DAN
(Snake)**

A R A M E A

Kedesh

Lake
Huleh

Hazor

B A S H A N

**NAPHTALI
(Gazelle)**

R. Jordan

The Bible Lands of Canaan as
they were divided among the
Twelve Tribes, with the six
Cities of Refuge and the five
cities of the Philistines. Each of
the Twelve Tribes is shown with
its traditional symbol. Travelers
could not cross the deserts of
Arabia between Egypt and
Mesopotamia, two of the
greatest markets of ancient
times. Instead they had to
journey through Canaan. The
ports of Byblos, Sidon (not
shown on map), and Tyre
belonged to the Phoenicians.

Sea of
Chinnereth
(Galilee)

Golan

**ZEBULUN
(Ship)**

R. Kishon

Nazareth

R. Yarmuk

Plain of Jezreel

**ISSACHAR
(Ass)**

Ramoth-Gilead

Taanach

G I L E A D

**MANASSEH
(Unicorn)**

R. Jordan

A M M O N

Shechem

R. Jabbok

🏰 Six cities of refuge

◼ Five cities of the
Philistines

**EPHRAIM
(Cattle)**

**GAD
(Tents)**

Rabbah

Joppa

Bethel

The Desert

**BENJAMIN
(Wolf)**

Mizpah

Jericho

Jerusalem

Bezer

Ashdod  Ekron

Askelon

**JUDAH
(Lion)**

Bethlehem

**REUBEN
(Mandrake)**

Gaza

P H I L I S T I A

Dead
Sea

Hebron

Gath

**SIMEON
(Castle)**

M O A B

A M A L E K   Debir   N e g e b   E D O M

# China and India

Farming in China began in the north on the plains around the Hwang-ho or Yellow River. Soon farming spread south to the plains of the Yangtze River. First villages, and then towns grew up along the river banks. Chinese crafts were sent westward along what became known as the "Silk Road," because so much silk cloth was taken from China to the west. For a long time the Chinese were the only people who knew how to produce silk. They could also make paper and they invented a form of money to help them in their trading.

Chinese history begins with the Shang dynasty (ruling family) which came to power in about 1500 B.C. The vast Chinese Empire was organized by a great army of civil servants who made sure that laws and taxes, weights and measures were the same all over the Empire. They also controlled the production of salt and the making of iron. Iron-working began in China in the 600s B.C. The metal was melted and cast in molds, not shaped by heating and hammering as in other places. It was another 1800 years before people in Europe began to cast iron!

In India, people learned to use the water of the river Indus to make their soil rich and bring them good crops and wealth. The Indus Valley people built a great system of dams and canals. By about 2500 B.C. they too began to live in cities. The greatest of the Indus Valley cities were Mohenjo Daro and Harappa, and there were certainly at least a hundred smaller towns and villages.

The cities lasted about 1,000 years, then they were deserted and forgotten. No one knows what happened. In Mohenjo Daro piles of clay missiles were found on the walls. These were probably ammunition for slings. Perhaps the city was attacked. Many unburied bodies were found in the streets. Perhaps the people died when the city was taken.

About the time Mohenjo Daro fell, new people known as Aryans arrived from the northwest and settled in northern India. They spread slowly east and south. By about 1000 B.C. they knew how to work iron, which is a very hard metal and difficult to use. During this time India itself was divided into many separate kingdoms, each ruled by a fortress-city surrounded by high walls and moats.

The Great Wall of China was built by the first Ch'in emperor in about 214 B.C. to defend his empire against the nomadic Huns in the north. The wall was nearly 3,000 miles long.

By 1500 B.C. the first Indian civilization, based in the Indus Valley, had disappeared. Excavation of its great centers at Harappa and Mohenjo Daro (below) has shown how highly organized it was.

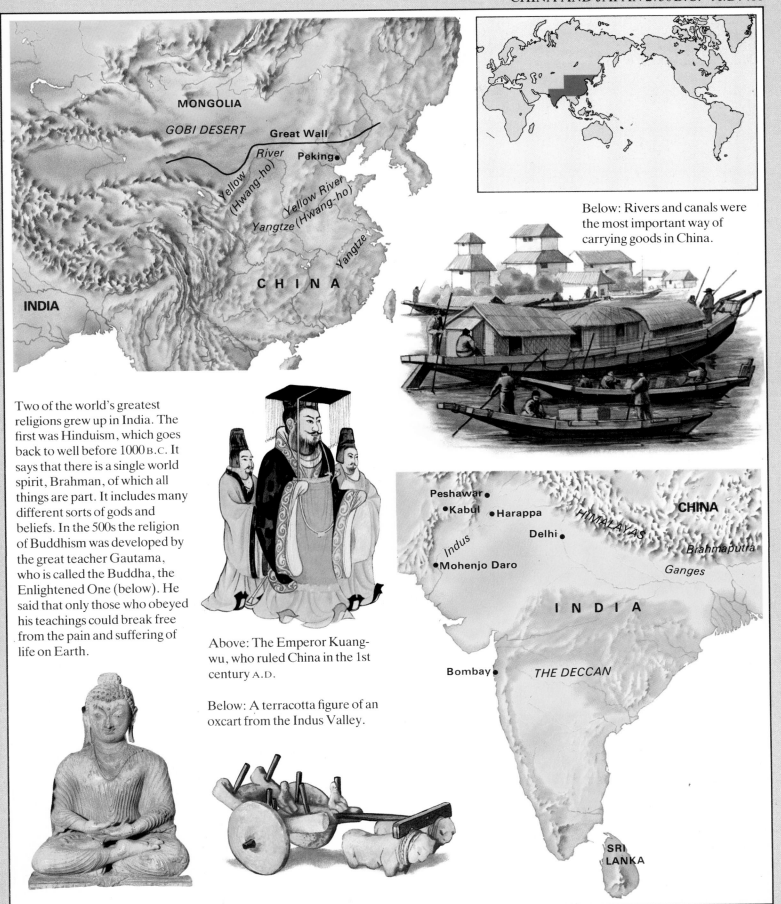

Below: Rivers and canals were the most important way of carrying goods in China.

Two of the world's greatest religions grew up in India. The first was Hinduism, which goes back to well before 1000 B.C. It says that there is a single world spirit, Brahman, of which all things are part. It includes many different sorts of gods and beliefs. In the 500s the religion of Buddhism was developed by the great teacher Gautama, who is called the Buddha, the Enlightened One (below). He said that only those who obeyed his teachings could break free from the pain and suffering of life on Earth.

Above: The Emperor Kuang-wu, who ruled China in the 1st century A.D.

Below: A terracotta figure of an oxcart from the Indus Valley.

# Ancient Greece

Northwest of Egypt lies the Aegean Sea. It is dotted with rocky islands, and on either side are two mountainous countries: mainland Greece on the west, and Anatolia (modern Turkey) on the east. The cities of the Aegean area were built on small pockets of farmland along the coast. It was easier to travel by sea than overland across the mountains, and the Greeks became good sailors. Soon they came to rely more and more on trading for a living.

The largest island in the Aegean is Crete. The people of Crete are known as Minoans, after their legendary King Minos. They were the first in this area to grow rich. They traded their goods with Egypt and other Mediterranean peoples. But suddenly, in about 1450 B.C., some disaster came to Crete. No one knows what happened, although the explosion of the volcano on the nearby island of Thera may have had something to do with it. The palaces were abandoned except for Knossos, which was taken over by the Mycenaeans.

The Mycenaeans came from mainland Greece. They took over many Minoan ways of life and became the most important traders in the Mediterranean. But soon there came a very troubled time in the whole eastern Mediterranean. Cities were destroyed and pirates roamed the area.

By the 900s B.C., there were small Greek cities on most of the Aegean islands, in Greece itself, and on the coasts of Anatolia. They were linked by having the same language and customs. As they grew rich they organized themselves into "city-states," made up of a main city, some villages, and the land around. Each city had its own army and citizens were expected to fight for their city and to provide their own armor and weapons. But the Greeks were not just soldiers. The elegant Greek buildings and statues are still admired and their careful studies were the beginnings of many modern sciences.

Above: The acropolis at Athens with the Parthenon, the great temple to the goddess Athena, in the foreground. It was built between 447 and 432 B.C. The city of Athens was one of the richest and most powerful states and had a strong navy.

Below: The Greek amphitheatre at Taormina in Sicily. The Greeks were the first people to write plays, which they acted at religious festivals. They built theaters like this in many of their cities.

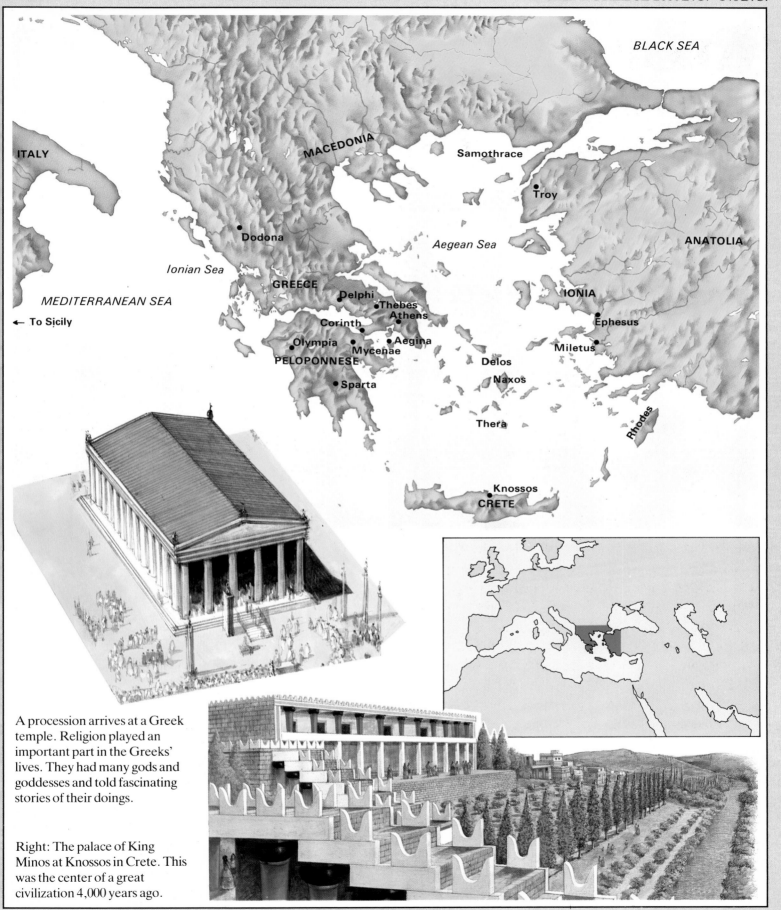

BLACK SEA

ITALY

MACEDONIA

Samothrace

Troy

ANATOLIA

Dodona

*Aegean Sea*

*Ionian Sea*

GREECE

Delphi

IONIA

MEDITERRANEAN SEA

← To Sicily

Corinth

Thebes
Athens

Ephesus

Olympia

Aegina

Miletus

Mycenae

PELOPONNESE

Delos

Sparta

Naxos

Thera

Rhodes

Knossos

CRETE

A procession arrives at a Greek temple. Religion played an important part in the Greeks' lives. They had many gods and goddesses and told fascinating stories of their doings.

Right: The palace of King Minos at Knossos in Crete. This was the center of a great civilization 4,000 years ago.

# Cyrus and Alexander

East of Mesopotamia, across the Zagros Mountains, lies the land that we now call Iran. It takes its name from nomads called Iranians who moved into the area in about 1300 B.C. Among the Iranians were two tribes called the Medes and the Persians and they grew more powerful than the others. In the 500s B.C. King Cyrus II of the Persians gained control of the whole area. At once he set out to build up a great empire.

The vast Empire was divided into 20 provinces and good roads were built to make it easier to travel. The greatest was the Royal Road, which stretched 1,600 miles from western Anatolia to Susa, the Persian capital.

The Greek cities of Anatolia were made part of the Persian Empire but mainland Greece fought off the Persian invasions. King Philip of Macedonia forced the Greek cities to join him for a great expedition to invade the Persian Empire. He was killed in 336 B.C., before he could see his dream come true. But his son Alexander crossed into Asia and in a few years had conquered the whole Persian Empire. He even invaded India. He hoped that the Greeks and Persians would become friends under his rule. But suddenly he died of fever. The generals who had served him so faithfully turned on one another and divided the Empire between themselves. Under these kingdoms Greek customs spread and lasted long after the kingdoms fell.

In the 500s B.C. King Darius of Persia began to build a great palace at Persepolis. His son Xerxes carried on the work, and when it was finished it was the finest of all the royal palaces. On the stairways of the huge hall are carvings showing groups of people from all over the Empire, bringing their gifts to the king. The picture above shows a few of them.

Right: Ruins of the Ancient Greek city of Ephesus, in Anatolia. The eastern Greek cities, freed from the Persians by Alexander in 333 B.C., rose in renewed splendor.

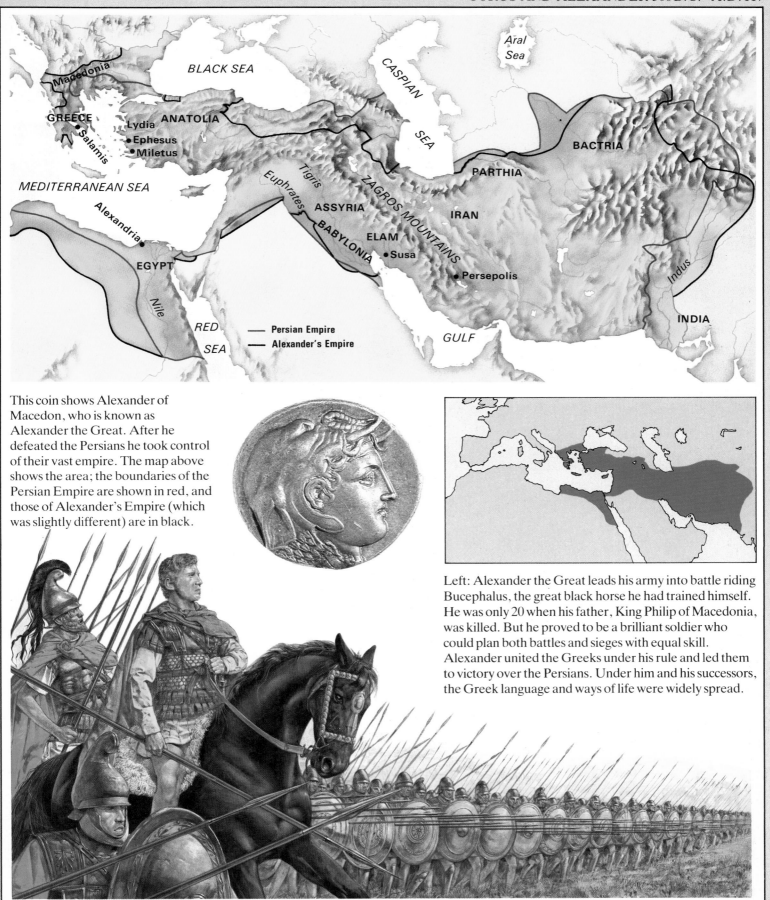

This coin shows Alexander of Macedon, who is known as Alexander the Great. After he defeated the Persians he took control of their vast empire. The map above shows the area; the boundaries of the Persian Empire are shown in red, and those of Alexander's Empire (which was slightly different) are in black.

Left: Alexander the Great leads his army into battle riding Bucephalus, the great black horse he had trained himself. He was only 20 when his father, King Philip of Macedonia, was killed. But he proved to be a brilliant soldier who could plan both battles and sieges with equal skill. Alexander united the Greeks under his rule and led them to victory over the Persians. Under him and his successors, the Greek language and ways of life were widely spread.

# Travel and Trade

In ancient times travel was a slow, difficult and often dangerous undertaking. On land, almost everyone journeyed on foot. They walked along rough tracks, and merchants packed their goods on to the backs of donkeys. There were few roads in Europe before the Romans built them, while in China the roads were for the use of government officials. After about 1600 B.C. people began to use horses to ride and to draw chariots, and later camels to carry loads. Oxen pulled heavy carts, but these were very slow and got bogged down in the mud. Wherever it was possible, goods were carried by water.

At first traders had to barter, exchanging goods that they agreed were of equal value. Then, by about 600 B.C., coins began to be used in the country of Lydia in Anatolia. Soon people all over the Mediterranean area were using them.

People usually wanted to exchange something they had plenty of, such as food or goods made by craftsmen, for some important necessity such as timber or metals which they lacked. If they had most of the things they needed in their own country, they could afford to buy luxuries like jewels and perfumes. Sometimes these came from far away. The blue stone called lapis lazuli was found only in Afghanistan, but it was traded all over the Mediterranean area. Cyprus takes its name from the copper found there, while Arabia produced resins, like frankincense, which gave off fragrant smells when they were burned. Gold came from southern Egypt and silver, copper, and tin from Spain.

By the A.D. 100s there was a great deal of trade between Europe and Asia, much of it through Arab ships which sailed across the Indian Ocean, carrying glass, metals, cloth, and pottery to exchange for silk, spices, and precious stones. Caravans traveled right across central Asia, linking the great empires of Rome and China.

The Romans built excellent roads, along which carts like the one below could travel. Most were pulled by oxen, which were strong but very slow. Horse collars had not yet been invented, which meant that horses pulling heavy loads would half strangle themselves if they went too fast.

This Egyptian tomb-painting dates from about 1400 B.C. It shows a heavily laden boat. Boats and ships were very important means of transport in the Ancient World, when there were few good roads. Travel by river or by sea was easier and cheaper than travel overland.

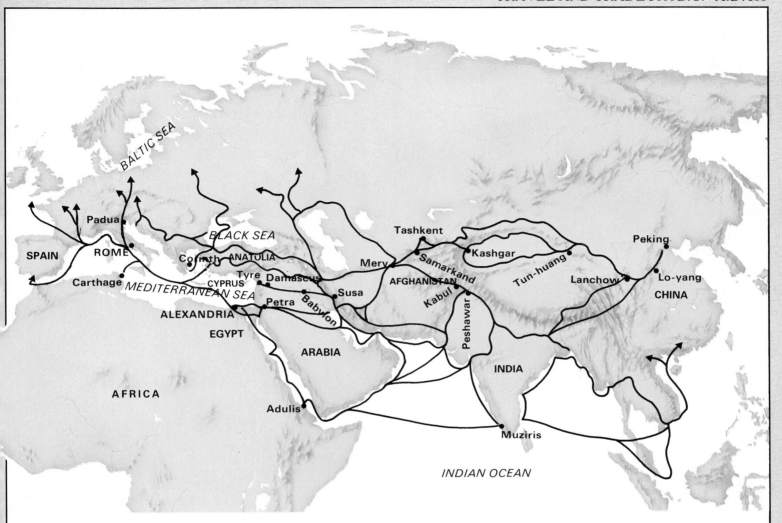

Map labels: BALTIC SEA, Padua, SPAIN, ROME, Carthage, MEDITERRANEAN SEA, BLACK SEA, Corinth, ANATOLIA, CYPRUS, Tyre, Damascus, ALEXANDRIA, EGYPT, Petra, Babylon, Susa, ARABIA, Mery, AFGHANISTAN, Kabul, Peshawar, Tashkent, Samarkand, Kashgar, Tun-huang, Lanchow, Peking, Lo-yang, CHINA, INDIA, AFRICA, Adulis, Muziris, INDIAN OCEAN

Above: The map shows many of the ancient trading routes. They stretch from Spain in the west to Peking in China in the east.

Below: Carthaginians beside their ship. Vessels like this were used for long sea journeys. In the 400s B.C. a Carthaginian called Hanno sailed from Carthage through the Strait of Gibraltar, and then turned south down the coast of Africa. He describes rivers teaming with crocodiles and hippopotamuses, volcanoes, and even gorillas. The Carthaginians traded for gold with the Africans. Carthage was a Phoenician colony on the north coast of Africa and became so powerful that at one time it looked as if it might overcome Rome itself.

## Travel by Water

The Chinese built a network of canals which joined their main rivers. The Tigris and Euphrates in Mesopotamia and the Nile in Egypt, were all busy waterways. The early Egyptians and Mesopotamians built boats out of the reeds that grew in the rivers. Boats were sometimes made of animal hides, and rafts were floated on blown-up animal skins. Sea-going craft were made of wood. The best timber came from the area on the east Mediterranean coast now called the Lebanon, where forests of great cedar trees grew. People from all over the Middle East came to buy it. Whenever possible, ships sailed within sight of land. If they had to cross open sea, they steered by the stars. Ships usually only sailed at times of year when they were likely to get good weather. The most famous sailors were the Greeks and Phoenicians. They built ships with more than one bank of oars on each side, and sailed to the British Isles, India, and around Africa, exploring and seeking trade.

# Rome and its Empire

The empire of Rome was the largest, and the last, of the Ancient World. According to one story, the city of Rome was founded in 753 B.C. by twins called Romulus and Remus. At first, kings ruled Rome, but they made themselves so unpopular that the Romans drove them out and set up a republic with an assembly for the citizens, a senate of nobles, and two consuls elected each year to lead them.

Rome had to fight its neighbors to survive, and every male citizen was a soldier. The Romans were so successful that they conquered all Italy. The other nations around the Mediterranean became suspicious of Rome. They had to be defeated, and then the Romans had to fight more wars to protect what they had won. In a short time Rome built up a great empire. To do this, the Romans had to reorganize their army, turning it into a well-trained force. They built towns and cities, and networks of good roads to link them, and introduced new and better ways of farming.

The Romans were very good at running their Empire. They spread their laws, taxes, and systems of government through the countries they ruled, and a Roman town in northern Europe was very like one in north Africa. It was built on the same pattern and the people there wore Roman clothes and spoke Latin, the Roman language.

The vast size of the Roman Empire was its undoing. It was too big for one man to rule over and its borders were too long for the armies to defend. The Roman Empire was divided into two: the Western Empire ruled from Rome, and the Eastern Empire ruled from Constantinople (also known as Byzantium). Friendly barbarian tribes were brought into its armies to help in its defense. But this could not save it. Other barbarian tribes invaded. The Eastern Empire managed to bribe them to go away, but the Empire in the west was overrun. The close links between the countries around the Mediterranean were broken for ever.

Above: This great arch stands among the ruins of Djemila, in Algeria, north Africa. It was built by the Romans in A.D. 216 and was once a thriving Roman town.
Left: The Colosseum in Rome was completed in A.D. 80. The amphitheater was built to hold 50,000 spectators.

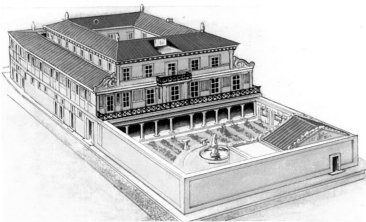

Left: A Roman villa in a town. It was built around a central courtyard. There was also a garden. Rooms on the ground floor looked on to the courtyard or the garden. The rooms that opened onto the street were let out as shops.

Left: A Roman soldier and his equipment. The soldiers complained that carrying so much made them no better than mules! Even so, Roman legions could march 30 miles a day, for many days at a time. They marched across the Empire, living in tents or in forts of stone or wood like the one below.

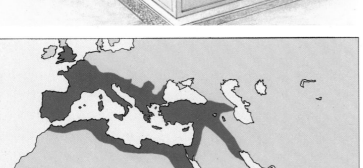

Below: The Roman Empire at its greatest, in A.D. 116. At this time it was ruled by the Emperor Trajan, a Spanish general who reigned for 19 years.

BRITAIN

Rhine

GAUL

Danube

DACIA

Danube

BLACK SEA

SPAIN

ITALY

Rome

Byzantium
(Constantinople)

ANATOLIA
(ASIA MINOR)

MESOPOTAMIA

Tigris

Athens

SYRIA

Euphrates

ALGERIA

Carthage

MEDITERRANEAN SEA

Jerusalem

AFRICA

Alexandria

EGYPT

Nile

RED SEA

# THE MIDDLE AGES

The great Roman Empire ruled the lands all around the Mediterranean Sea. It linked them with common laws and language. Traders sailed across the Mediterranean and traveled along the network of roads that spread all over the Empire. All this was changed when the barbarians overran the western half of the Roman Empire and its emperor gave up his throne in A.D. 476. The next thousand years are known as the Middle Ages, and during them the lands south and east of the Mediterranean developed in quite different ways from western Europe.

**The Americas**
- The Mayan civilization in Yucatan, Mexico (5) reached its height around A.D. 600. The ceremonial centers in the lowlands collapsed and Chichen Itza in the highlands gained importance. In about A.D. 900 the civilization ended as palaces and villages were abandoned.
- The Incas became established on parts of the South American Pacific coast in the 400s but it was not until the 1400s that their empire was established in Peru (6).
- The Toltecs existed in Mexico (4) until their empire collapsed in 1151.
- The 1300s saw the rise of the Aztecs and their city of Tenochtitlán in Mexico (3).
- In the north, Leif Eriksson and the Vikings reached the coast of North America (1) in about 1000.
- North American Indians had settled in parts of North America (2).

**Africa**
- By 800 the kingdom of Ghana (8), south of the Sahara, was a major trading state and was converted to Islam.
- In about 1100 the building of Greater Zimbabwe (10) began.
- In the West African forest kingdoms (7) the Ife produced terracotta and bronze figures.
- At Lalibela in Ethiopia (11) churches were carved out of the solid rock.
- Mali (9), just south of the Sahara, expanded.

**The Near East**
- In 570 the Prophet Muhammad was born in Mecca (12) in Arabia. He founded the religion of Islam which spread with astonishing speed through the Near East. It then spread from Spain and Portugal (16) in the west through North Africa to the borders of India (28).
- Crusaders conquered the Holy Land (13) but the Muslims fought back and regained the area.
- The Byzantine Empire (Eastern Roman Empire) gradually lost its power. In 1071 Anatolia (modern Turkey) (14) fell to the Turks, and the Byzantine lands of Italy and Sicily were taken by the Normans. Constantinople (15) and the land around it was captured by the Turks in 1453.

## Western Europe

● The Western Roman Empire fell under barbarian rule. The Franks gained control of much of modern France (17) and Germany (18). Charlemagne led the Franks and was crowned Roman Emperor in 800.

● Vikings from Scandinavia (22) raided and plundered the British Isles (21) and the northern coast of mainland Europe, later settling there as farmers. They also colonized Iceland (20).

● In 871 Alfred the Great became King of Wessex. He defeated the Danes and stopped them spreading into the west of England (19).

● In 962 the Holy Roman Empire was revived by Otto I of Germany (18).

● In 1066 William of Normandy conquered England (19) and it was organized under the feudal system, as was France (17).

● Christianity spread and the Church played a very important part in everyday and political life.

● In 1337 the Hundred Years' War between England and France began.

● In 1348 a terrible plague called the Black Death spread through Europe and killed thousands.

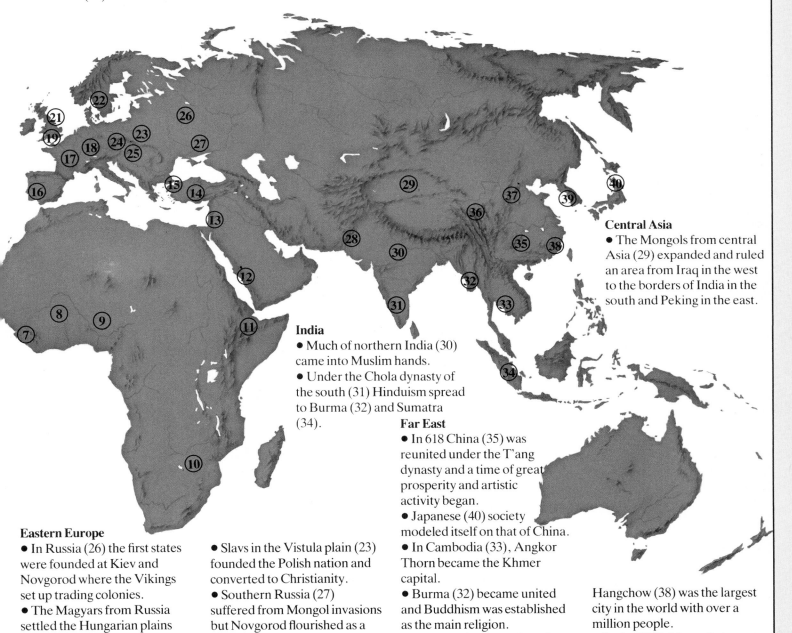

## Central Asia

● The Mongols from central Asia (29) expanded and ruled an area from Iraq in the west to the borders of India in the south and Peking in the east.

## India

● Much of northern India (30) came into Muslim hands.

● Under the Chola dynasty of the south (31) Hinduism spread to Burma (32) and Sumatra (34).

## Far East

● In 618 China (35) was reunited under the T'ang dynasty and a time of great prosperity and artistic activity began.

● Japanese (40) society modeled itself on that of China.

● In Cambodia (33), Angkor Thorn became the Khmer capital.

● Burma (32) became united and Buddhism was established as the main religion.

● Mongols dominated northern China (36) and Korea (39). Meanwhile, in the south,

## Eastern Europe

● In Russia (26) the first states were founded at Kiev and Novgorod where the Vikings set up trading colonies.

● The Magyars from Russia settled the Hungarian plains (25) and St. Stephen centralized government and introduced Christianity.

● Slavs in the Vistula plain (23) founded the Polish nation and converted to Christianity.

● Southern Russia (27) suffered from Mongol invasions but Novgorod flourished as a free republic.

● The Czech kingdom of Bohemia (24) flourished.

Hangchow (38) was the largest city in the world with over a million people.

● In the 1270s Marco Polo reached the Mongol court at Peking (37).

# The Barbarians

In the A.D. 400s barbarian tribes from east of the Danube and Volga rivers were attacked by the Huns from central Asia. They fled across the frontiers and into the Roman Empire where they settled. The barbarians were farmers and they set up their own kingdoms with villages of wooden houses. They were also great fighters. Bands of robbers made it difficult to travel and there was little trade over long distances. Europe changed from being part of one great empire into a patchwork of little kingdoms.

One of the barbarian tribes to settle inside the Roman Empire was the Franks. By A.D. 500 they ruled over a huge kingdom including much of modern France and West Germany. The greatest king of the Franks was Charlemagne, who came to the throne in 768. He brought the neighboring countries under his control and then fought against the Saxons and Slavs in the east. He forced the people he conquered to become Christians. In 800 the Pope crowned him "Holy Roman Emperor."

Two other great waves of invasion troubled western Europe in the early Middle Ages. In the late 700s the people on the northern coasts were terrified by raiders from the sea. They were the Vikings from Denmark, Sweden, and Norway.

For the next 200 years bands of up to 400 raiders plundered towns and monasteries. But they were not all raiders. Some became farmers and settled in Britain and France.

In the late 800s about 25,000 Magyars moved from central Asia to settle in the Hungarian Plains. From there they raided Germany, Italy, and France. In 955 the Emperor Otto I defeated them at the battle of Lech. After this they settled down in Hungary and became farmers, and soon many became Christians.

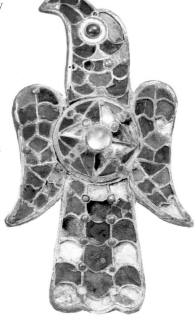

Right: This brooch was made by an Ostrogoth in the late 400s. It is made of gold and precious stones. The barbarians loved jewelry and were very skilled metal workers.

Below left: The Oseberg ship. The splendid Viking ships that were once used for royal burials are today carefully preserved in special museums.

Below: Part of a reconstruction of a tapestry found on the Oseberg ship. The figures shown here, with their wagons and horses, may be taking part in some kind of burial ceremony.

FINNS

NORSE     SWEDES     Volga

PICTS

IRISH     NORTH
          SEA        JUTES     ANGLES     BALTS

          BRITISH                         SLAVS
          ANGLO-    ANGLES
London ●  SAXONS   FRISIANS   SAXONS      SLAVS
English Channel              THURINGIANS

BRETONS            Rhine
          ● Paris  ALAMANNI   RUGIANS              HUNS        ALANS
FRANKS    BURGUNDIANS                  LOMBARDS                HUNS
BAY OF             Lech ●                          GOTHS
BISCAY                               GEPIDS
SUEVI                       OSTROGOTHS            BLACK SEA
     BASQUES
                                     Danube
     VISIGOTHS
                    ● Rome      Constantinople
                                (Byzantium) ●

                                EASTERN ROMAN EMPIRE

          VANDALS

                    MEDITERRANEAN SEA

     BERBERS

The map above shows where the different barbarian tribes were living in 476, the year when the last emperor in the west gave up his throne. In the 400s and 500s the tribes shifted around. The Anglo-Saxons moved north and west across Britain, for example. The barbarians built villages of wooden houses, like the ones in the picture on the right.

The Vikings were great traders as well as raiders. They set up trading colonies in Russia and farming and trading settlements in Greenland and Iceland. They reached America, where they traded for timber and furs.

GREENLAND     ICELAND

AMERICA                              RUSSIA

     ⌁ Viking journeys
     - - - probable Viking journeys
     ■ Viking homelands
     ▨ Viking settlements

# The Spread of Christianity

Jesus Christ was born about 1988 years ago in the Roman province of Judea during the reign of King Herod the Great. After he was killed by the Romans when he was about 30 years old, his followers traveled all through the Roman Empire preaching and forming groups of Christians.

Many of the early Christians were killed because they refused to worship the Roman emperor as a god. But then, about 300 years after Jesus died, the Roman emperor himself became a Christian. Thousands of other Romans followed his example and Christianity became the official religion of the Empire.

There were many quarrels among the Christians. The Christians in western Europe looked on the Bishop of Rome—the Pope—as their leader, while those in the eastern part of the Empire were led by the head of the Church in Constantinople. In the end the western and eastern Christians split into the Roman Catholic Church and the Eastern Orthodox Church.

When the barbarians overran western Europe in the A.D. 400s the organization of the Roman Empire broke down. As a result, the Christians became very important. Churchmen were often the only people who could read and write and who had any experience in administration. The Church was the one strong link between the different barbarian kingdoms.

Many Christians gathered together to live in monasteries and convents. Other Christians became missionaries and spent most of their time traveling and spreading their faith. However, it was a long time before all Europe was Christian.

Above: This stained glass was made in Germany in the 1400s. It shows St. Bernard reaping in the fields. St. Bernard was the abbot of Clairvaux in France in the 1100s and was responsible for founding many other monasteries.

Right: This jeweled cross dates from about A.D. 1000. It comes from Constantinople. In the center is the Virgin Mary with St. Basil and St. Gregory on either side.

Left: A 12th-century mosaic of Jesus Christ. This Byzantine mosaic is in Monreale Abbey Church in Sicily.

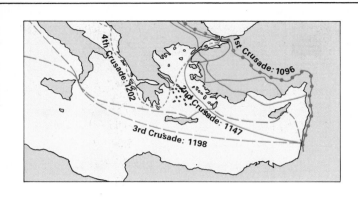

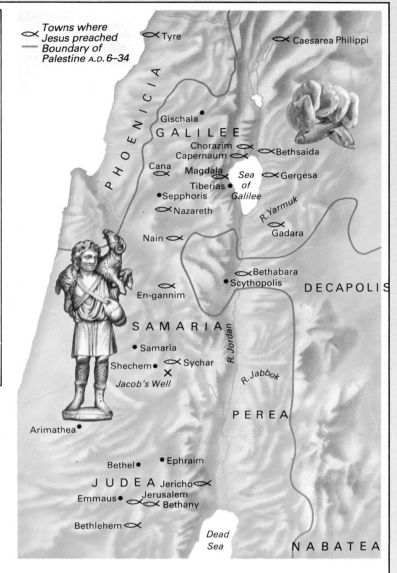

Towns where Jesus preached
Boundary of Palestine A.D. 6–34

## The Crusades

Between 1096 and 1270 Christian armies from Europe set out to recapture Jerusalem and the Holy Land from the Muslims. They firmly believed that Christ's birthplace should be in Christian hands. The first crusade, as these holy wars were called, was a great success, but soon the Muslim Turks fought back. Several more crusades were called, but without success. The map above shows the routes taken by Crusaders on the first four crusades.

Right: Palestine at the time when Jesus lived. It shows the towns where he preached. Inset are the five loaves and two fishes of the Miracle at Bethsaida and an early Christian statue picturing Jesus as the Good Shepherd with a lamb.

Below: The spread of Christianity through Europe and the Middle East. The dotted area shows how far it had spread by A.D. 600. Much of this was later conquered by the Muslims. The Eastern Orthodox, or Byzantine, Church grew away from the Roman Church and split from it in 1054. Russia became Orthodox, but most of central Europe was converted by missionaries from the Roman Church.

Strongly Christian in 325
Roman Catholic, 900
Roman Catholic, 1096
Eastern Orthodox, 900
Eastern Orthodox, 1096
Christian by 600

# The Rise of Islam

In the A.D. 600s a great new religion began. It is called *Islam*, which means "Submission to the Will of Allah" (God), and the people who believe in it are called Muslims. In less than a hundred years the Muslims spread out from the town of Mecca in Arabia to rule an empire that stretched from Spain in the west, to India in the east.

The Muslims borrowed and improved on the best ideas of the peoples they conquered. They translated the works of the Ancient Greeks into Arabic, and learned what they had known of medicine, mathematics, astronomy, and mechanics. Their traders learned how to make paper from the Chinese and how to write down numbers with nine digits and a zero from the Indians.

All over the Muslim Empire people lived in the same sort of way, for the teachings of Islam laid down many rules for everyday life. People could travel safely from one end of the great Empire to the other, so trading became safe and easy. The spread of the Arabic language meant that merchants from different countries could understand one another and a single kind of gold coin, the dinar, was used throughout the Empire.

For the first few years the Muslim lands were ruled by a single *caliph*. But then many provinces broke away to be ruled by their own *sultans*. The most important of these were Turks. The Turks were nomads from central Asia, who first came into the Islamic world as slaves. Then they became Muslims and the Empire's most important soldiers. They soon gained control of much of the Middle East and moved north to the Byzantine Empire. They settled in Anatolia, which is now called Turkey after them. The most important Turks were the Ottomans. Slowly they won control of the old Byzantine Empire until only the Byzantine capital, Constantinople, and a little land around it remained. In 1453 the Turks captured even this last stronghold.

Soon the Ottomans ruled over a Muslim empire from Algeria to Iraq. They controlled much of the Mediterranean shipping. Several times they invaded Europe and even threatened the Holy Roman Empire's capital, Vienna. They kept the Empire together by an efficient system of government, with officials in every village. But above all, it was held together by the Muslim faith.

### The Prophet Muhammad

The religion of Islam was founded by the Prophet Muhammad. Muslims believe that the angel Gabriel appeared to Muhammad and told him Allah's commands and teachings, which he passed on to his companions. Later they were collected into a single book, the *Koran*, which is the holy book of the Muslims. Muslims share many beliefs with Jews and Christians, and honor the great Jewish prophets. They respect Christ as a great prophet, but do not believe that he is God. At first few people believed Muhammad's teachings, but before he died he had gained many followers. Muslim rule spread quickly, and with it spread the language of Arabic, in which the *Koran* was written.

This painting shows Muhammad with his followers before the battle of Uhad. There was no water and in a miracle water streamed from the Prophet's fingers. Muslim artists are forbidden to show Muhammad's face, so it has been veiled.

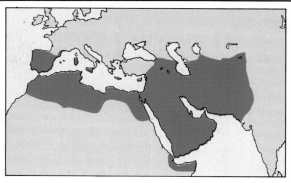

Left: This picture was painted in Baghdad in 1237. It shows a trader about to mount his camel and set off on an expedition. Merchants traveled all over the Islamic Empire, carrying their goods on donkeys, camels, and mules roped together in processions called caravans. Arab merchants also controlled the trade from the East to Europe, which passed through Muslim lands.

Below: This map shows how the Muslims spread their religion through the southern Mediterranean and Middle East. They built up a vast empire in a very short time.

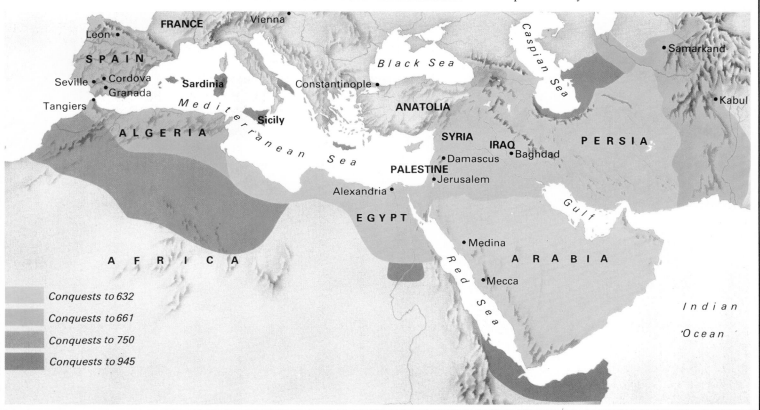

Conquests to 632
Conquests to 661
Conquests to 750
Conquests to 945

# Feudal Life

In Europe during the early Middle Ages, kings and chiefs did not have enough money or plunder to reward the men who fought for them. Instead, they rewarded them by giving them land. Out of this grew the "feudal system," because land given like this was called by the Latin word *feudum*.

Under the feudal system each state was ruled by a king or prince. He owned all the land, but gave large areas of it to his nobles. In return they promised that they and their men would fight for him when needed, be loyal and carry out certain other duties. From their castles nobles ruled the surrounding countryside.

Nobles divided up their large estates into smaller units called manors which they gave to knights on roughly the same terms as those between the noble and the king. On every manor there were peasants who worked the land. They had to work in their lord's fields for two or three days a week and they could not marry or leave the manor without his permission.

In the early days the feudal system worked quite well, particularly in France and England. But, gradually, all over Europe peasants revolted against their masters and in many countries feudal society was brought to an end. In central and eastern Europe, however, the feudal way of life lasted well into the 1800s.

### Life on the Land

Most of the village land was divided into three large fields. Each man held several strips of land, scattered across each field. It was usual to grow wheat in one field, barley in the second, and leave the third fallow (unsown) so that it could get back its goodness. Each year the crops were changed around and a different field was fallow. Each village had a large common where everyone was allowed to graze their sheep and cattle. It was a tough, hard life and people knew nothing of germs and diseases. In 1348 a new disease spread to Europe from the East. This was the Black Death and it is thought to have killed one person in every three. Whole villages were wiped out.

This picture was painted in the 1400s. It shows peasants at work on the land outside the great castle of Lusignan in western France. A peasant is plowing with a pair of oxen. Others are tending their vines and herding sheep. The picture comes from a "Book of Hours" painted for the Duke of Berry, the brother of the king of France, who was a great landowner.

Above: Europe in 1173. At this time the king of England ruled over more of France than the French king! Some of these lands had belonged to Duke William of Normandy, who conquered England in 1066. The rest had come through marriages. Spain was mostly ruled by Muslims, known as Moors.

Above: Europe in 1517. Spain and Portugal are now kingdoms. The English have lost their lands in France after defeat in the Hundred Years' War, which ended in 1453. Germany and Italy are still made up of many small states. Those in Germany are linked as the Holy Roman Empire.

Below: A castle under attack in the Middle Ages. In times of war peasants from the country around a castle would come with their animals to shelter inside its walls. Attackers surrounded the castle and tried to break into it in a number of ways. They battered the walls with huge rams and hurled stones at them with catapults.

They wheeled giant siege towers against the walls from which they could jump onto the castle. When all these efforts failed, the attackers camped outside and hoped to starve out the people inside. The defenders shot at them with arrows and dropped stones and boiling oil on them.

# The Mongol Empire

In the early 1200s a number of wandering tribes who lived in central Asia joined together under a new leader. They called him Genghis Khan, which meant "the very mighty lord." Under him and his family the Mongol tribes conquered a vast empire which stretched from China in the east to Hungary in the west.

The Mongols came from the steppes of Mongolia. Here there are wide treeless plains overlooked by snow-topped mountains. Winter is bitterly cold and in summer the burning sun turns the soil to dust while plants wither and die in the heat. The Mongols lived a nomadic life, moving around with their flocks and herds in search of grazing.

The Mongol Empire was too huge for one person to rule. In the late 1200s it was divided into four *Khanates*. But the Khans quarreled among themselves and the people they ruled over grew strong enough to drive them out.

In the 1240s the Mongol hordes poured through southern Russia, Poland, and Hungary. They burned down cities, killed thousands of people and laid waste the countryside. They easily defeated the slow-moving European soldiers sent against them. It seemed that only a miracle could stop them. Suddenly, they packed their tents and turned eastward. Their Great Khan Ogadei had died and they had been called back to vote for a new khan. Southern Russia was ruled by them for more than a hundred years to come, but the rest of Europe had been saved.

### Genghis Khan

Genghis Khan led his Mongol hordes (troops) first into China and then westward across central Asia. He soon learned how to attack cities that held out against him and break down their walls. A few craftsmen who would be useful were taken prisoner, but most people were killed and their heads cut off. People were so terrified of the Mongols that they often surrendered without fighting. Genghis Khan then did not harm them or their cities. Once the Mongols had conquered an area they were good rulers. The *Yasak*, as the Mongol laws were called, was obeyed all through the Empire. The Khan paid informers to tell him what was happening in distant places, and messengers called arrow riders carried his orders for 250 miles a day on relays of ponies. Trade went on busily, and travelers, merchants, and missionaries made journeys safely back and forth across Asia.

Left: Genghis Khan, the greatest of all Mongol leaders.

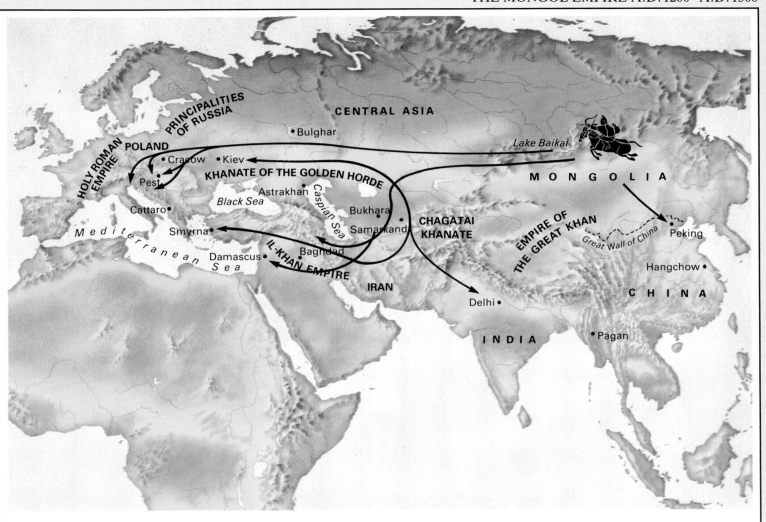

PRINCIPALITIES OF RUSSIA

CENTRAL ASIA

• Bulghar

*Lake Baikal*

M O N G O L I A

POLAND

HOLY ROMAN EMPIRE

• Cracow   • Kiev

Pest•

KHANATE OF THE GOLDEN HORDE

Cattaro•

*Black Sea*

Astrakhan •

*Caspian Sea*

Bukhara•

Samarkand•

CHAGATAI KHANATE

EMPIRE OF THE GREAT KHAN

*Great Wall of China*

• Peking

Smyrna•

*M e d i t e r r a n e a n*

Bagdad•

IL-KHAN EMPIRE

Damascus•

*Sea*

IRAN

Delhi •

Hangchow •

C H I N A

I N D I A

• Pagan

Above: The Mongol Empire stretched from China right into Europe. The Mongol armies traveled very quickly and usually took their enemies by surprise. The cities on the map are cities burned down by the Mongols, and the arrows show their main invasion routes.

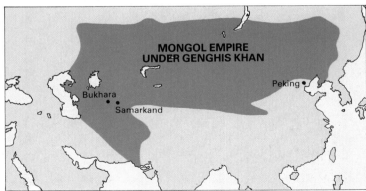

MONGOL EMPIRE UNDER GENGHIS KHAN

Bukhara•

Samarkand•

Peking•

The small map shows the extent of the Mongol Empire under Genghis Khan.

Left: A Mongol camp today. Now, as hundreds of years ago, the Mongols live in felt tents called *yurts*. They move around looking for grazing for their flocks and herds.

# Travel and Trade

When western Europe was overrun by the barbarians, it became cut off from the Mediterranean countries and their trade. In the Eastern Roman Empire and the Muslim countries, trade grew busier than ever, and more and more of it was with the East. Arab merchants traveled right across central Asia along routes like the Silk Road, which led from the Black Sea to China. Here they bought silk, porcelain, salt, and spices in return for gold and jade. Other Arabs went by sea to India and then eastward to the Spice Islands in the East Indies.

Meanwhile, trade in western Europe had slowed down. Travel was difficult and dangerous. The trade routes followed the old Roman roads, even though they were now just mud and gravel. Along them went soldiers, pilgrims, and merchants. Rich people traveled on horses but most people walked. Bandits lurked on lonely stretches of road, and no one dared travel after dark.

From northern Europe came grain and furs, flax and herring, copper and iron. England was specially famous for its wool. From southern Europe came wine and olives. For many years the Italians had almost complete control of the trade with the East. Gradually other European merchants became bolder and began to travel farther and farther to the south and east.

Above right: Princess Isabella of France goes to meet her husband, King Richard II of England, in 1396. She travels in a splendid *litter*, supported by horses.

Center right: A group of merchants following the camels on which their goods are loaded. This painting comes from a map of central Asia and China made in about 1375. Its information came largely from the writings of Marco Polo (see opposite page).

Right: A market place in the 1400s. People from the countryside around would bring their goods to the local market town where they would sell them and buy what they could not produce themselves. Around the market place were streets of small shops with symbols hanging outside to show what they sold; a cobbler would hang out a shoe, for example. People who lived in towns were outside the feudal system. They were loyal to the king, or to the noble who had founded the town.

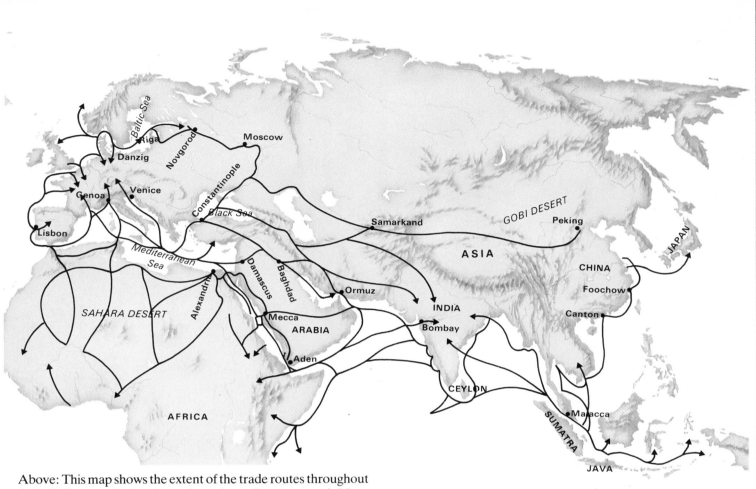

Above: This map shows the extent of the trade routes throughout the Middle Ages. It also shows the main trading towns and cities which grew up on good harbors along the coasts or inland where trade routes crossed.

## Marco Polo

In the late 1200s, Marco Polo, a merchant from Venice, spent several years traveling across Asia to Peking with his father and uncle. He traveled widely in the service of the great Mongol emperor, Kublai Khan. After 24 years he returned to Venice a wealthy man and wrote a book describing his travels and all the wonderful things he had seen. This book gave Europeans their first glimpse of China's wealth and culture.

# America before Columbus

The people of North America were mostly hunters, adding to their food supply by gathering roots, berries, and nuts. They built tents and shelters out of skins and branches. Some, like the Iroquois, who lived in the northeastern woodlands, became farmers. They built their wooden houses inside a palisade (fence) of tall wooden stakes which protected them from attack. Farther south, the Pueblo Indians built mud brick buildings like great apartment houses. These had hundreds of rooms built around a central courtyard, which were entered by holes in the roofs.

In Central and South America, in what are now Mexico and Peru, great empires grew up where people lived in cities as fine as many in Europe and the East. The Mayas lived in Yucatan in Central America. They were important from

Above: The Aztecs wrote records and histories in a kind of book which we call a *codex*. It was made of a single strip of leather, which was then folded up. The Aztecs wrote in *glyphs*—pictures which represent words. This picture shows part of a codex.

Below: The Inca city of Machu Picchu was built high in the Peruvian Andes mountains and surrounded by terraced fields where food could be grown. It was the last stronghold of the Incas who lingered on there after the Spanish conquest.

about A.D. 300 to about A.D. 900, when they abandoned palaces and villages. No one knows why. The Toltec Empire based around their capital city, Tula, existed from about A.D. 750 to about 1100. The Incas, who lived around Cuzco in the Andes, first began to grow powerful in the A.D. 1200s, but they did not conquer their enormous empire until the 1400s. The Aztecs, too, only controlled Mexico from the late 1400s. Both had their own customs, but their way of life was based on that of the earlier people of the area.

They grew corn and many local vegetables. Alpacas and llamas provided wool and carried heavy loads. Hunting, trapping, and fishing added to the larder. Ordinary houses were built of *adobe* (sun-dried mud bricks) or of stone. Great fortresses and monuments were made of stone.

In about A.D. 1000 some Vikings landed on the northeast coast, and for a time traded there. But until Christopher Columbus arrived in 1492, the Americas developed in a way which had nothing to do with Europe.

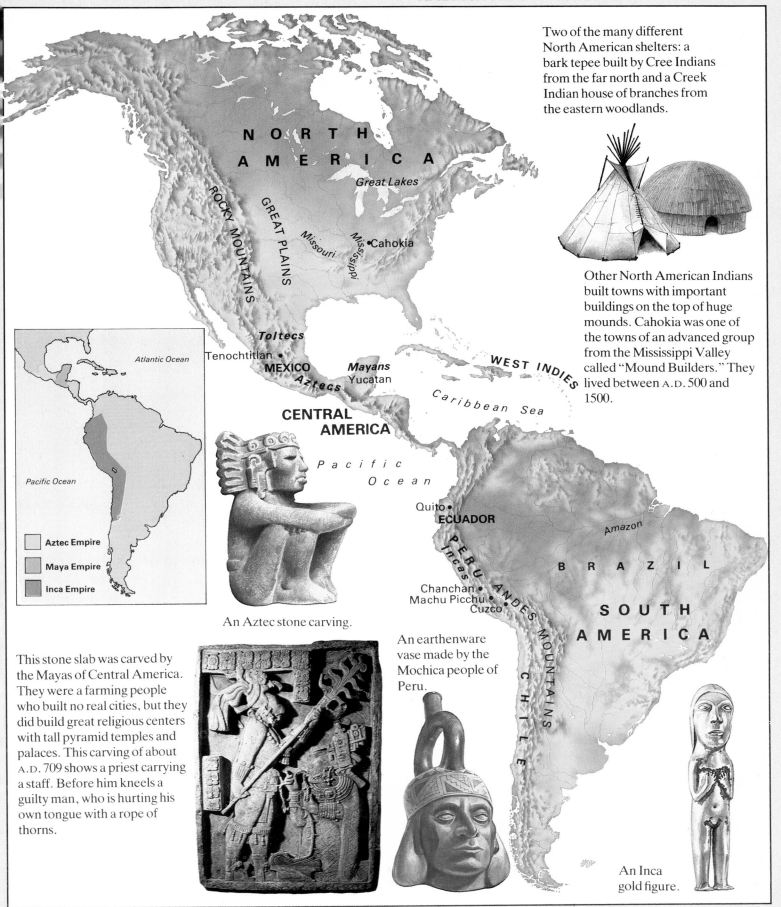

Two of the many different North American shelters: a bark tepee built by Cree Indians from the far north and a Creek Indian house of branches from the eastern woodlands.

Other North American Indians built towns with important buildings on the top of huge mounds. Cahokia was one of the towns of an advanced group from the Mississippi Valley called "Mound Builders." They lived between A.D. 500 and 1500.

NORTH AMERICA

Great Lakes

ROCKY MOUNTAINS

GREAT PLAINS

Missouri

Mississippi

•Cahokia

Toltecs

Tenochtitlan •

MEXICO

Aztecs

Mayans
Yucatan

WEST INDIES

Caribbean Sea

CENTRAL AMERICA

Pacific Ocean

Atlantic Ocean

Pacific Ocean

Aztec Empire
Maya Empire
Inca Empire

Quito •
ECUADOR

Amazon

Incas

PERU

Chanchan •
Machu Picchu •
Cuzco

ANDES MOUNTAINS

CHILE

BRAZIL

SOUTH AMERICA

An Aztec stone carving.

This stone slab was carved by the Mayas of Central America. They were a farming people who built no real cities, but they did build great religious centers with tall pyramid temples and palaces. This carving of about A.D. 709 shows a priest carrying a staff. Before him kneels a guilty man, who is hurting his own tongue with a rope of thorns.

An earthenware vase made by the Mochica people of Peru.

An Inca gold figure.

# THE AGE OF DISCOVERY

In the 1450s people in Europe and Asia did not know that the Americas and Australia existed. They did not even know that it was possible to sail south around the tip of Africa. But soon all this changed. The explorers were not the only people to make discoveries at this time. People were discovering again the knowledge of the Ancient Greeks and Romans which had been lost since the barbarians took over the Roman Empire a thousand years earlier. Printing was invented in Europe and during this time people began to question the teachings of the Church.

### The Americas
● In 1492 Christopher Columbus sailed across the Atlantic Ocean and reached the West Indies (3). Later he went on to the coast of Central America.
● The Aztec civilization in Mexico (4) and the Incas in Peru (6) were destroyed by the Spanish. Much of North and South America had been explored by the Spaniards who by 1550 had followed the Amazon from Peru to its mouth.
● The French were established in Canada after Jacques Cartier's journey up the St. Lawrence River (1) in 1535.
● The English, French, and Dutch had begun to colonize the Atlantic coast (2) of North America.

### Africa
● In the west the Benin Empire (11) was growing. The east coast (15) was settled by Muslim traders.
● In 1488 Bartolomeu Dias sailed around the southern tip of Africa (14) into the Indian Ocean.
● The Songhai Empire (9) on the Niger controlled the main trade routes across the Sahara Desert. The Portuguese set up trading posts (10) on the Gold Coast (Ghana) and in East Africa.
● The breakup of the Congo kingdom (12) had begun, as a result of war with Portugal.
● The Dutch, English, and French traded in slaves from West Africa (8) with the New World. In 1652 the Dutch East India Company set up a base at the Cape of Good Hope (13).

● Spanish colonies in Central and South America (5) sent vast quantities of silver and gold to Europe.
● Brazil (7) under the Portuguese, was important as a sugar producer.

### Europe
● The Hundred Years' War between England and France (23) ended in 1453 with the loss of almost all England's lands in France.
● The Italian Renaissance (19) soon spread northward.
● In 1519, the first ships to sail around the world set out from Europe (20) under Ferdinand Magellan.

### The Near East
● The Ottoman Turks captured Constantinople (18) in 1453. They were at the height of their power under Suleyman the Magnificent who captured much of Hungary after the battle of Mohacs (1526).
● The Turks dominated the Islamic world. They controlled not only Anatolia but also the Balkans in Europe, and Egypt, Syria and the Muslim holy cities of Mecca and Medina (16).
● The Safavids ruled Persia (17) but spent much time fighting their fellow Muslims, the Ottoman Turks.
● Persia declined after a peak under Safavid Shah Abbas the Great (1587–1629).

## Europe
- In Germany (25) Gutenberg invented his printing process and Luther began the Reformation by setting up a "reformed" Protestant Church. Lutheranism spread over most of northern Germany and Scandinavia (27). The ideas of John Calvin, another Protestant reformer, spread from his native Geneva (24) to Scotland, France and the Netherlands.
- In Italy, the Council of Trent (1545–1563) was set up to strengthen the Catholic Church in its struggle against Protestantism.
- France (23) suffered from religious wars between the Catholics and Protestants (Huguenots) from 1562 to 1598.
- England at war with Spain. In 1588 England defeated the Spanish Armada.
- Portugal (21) regained independence in 1640 after 60 years of Spanish rule.
- Civil War in England (22) ended in the execution of Charles I (1649) and the setting up of a Commonwealth (Republic).
- In the Baltic region Sweden (26) was the leading power.

## Russia
- The Mongols controlled much of Russia (28).
- Moscow (29) grew powerful after 1462 under Ivan the Great. Russia continued to expand at the expense of the Muslim Khanates on the river Volga (30) under Ivan IV (the Terrible).
- The Russian conquest of Siberia (31) began. Cossacks and traders crossed the Urals and reached the Pacific at Okhotsk (32).

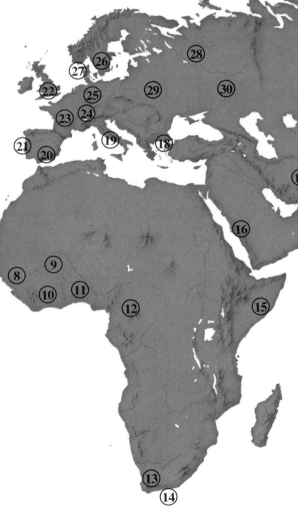

## India
- In 1526 the Muslim Mongols set up the Mughal Empire in the north (35); Hindu kingdoms remained in the south (36). Arabs still dominated trade on the west coast. The Mughal Empire expanded under Akbar, its greatest emperor, to cover most of north and central India. The Taj Mahal, built by Emperor Shah Janan in memory of his wife, was completed in 1653.

## The Far East
- China (34) revived under the Ming dynasty.
- The Manchus captured Peking and set up a new dynasty, the Ch'ing. It ruled China until the 20th century.
- Japan (33) was torn by civil war.
- The Tokugawa family ruled Japan (until 1868); Japanese were not allowed to go abroad or build ocean-going ships.
- The Dutch drove the Portuguese from the Spice Islands (37) and made Batavia (Djakarta) the capital of their empire.

## The Pacific
- In 1768 Captain James Cook set out to explore the Pacific. He claimed New Zealand (39) and eastern Australia (38) for Britain.

# The Great Explorers

In the 1400s Portuguese sailors began to sail farther and farther down the west coast of Africa. They were helped by a group of mapmakers and astronomers, pilots, and ship designers, who had been brought together by Prince Henry of Portugal. He is known as Prince Henry the Navigator. The first person to round the tip of Africa was Bartolomeu Dias, in 1487. Ten years later Vasco da Gama set out from Portugal to sail to the East.

Meanwhile, other explorers decided to try to reach the Spice Islands in the East Indies by sailing west. They never dreamed that a huge continent lay in their way. In 1492 Christopher Columbus, an Italian working for the Spanish queen, set out with three little ships. After sailing for more than a month he reached the islands of the West Indies. He made four voyages altogether, sailing through the islands to the coasts of South and Central America. To the end of his life,

he believed he had reached Asia; and this is why those islands are named the West Indies, and the people there and on the mainland of America became known as Indians.

Within a few years, other explorers sailed to America and people began to realize the truth. A vast new continent had been discovered. It was named after the explorer Amerigo Vespucci who sailed far down the coast of Brazil. In 1519 Ferdinand Magellan set out from Spain with five old ships. When he reached America he turned south and then west through the strait which is called after him. Magellan's ships sailed on across the open sea to the Philippines. There he was killed in a fight with the islanders. Only one ship of his five finally reached Spain, nearly three years later. It had made the first journey around the world, but it had also shown that the westward route to the Spice Islands was far too difficult and dangerous for ordinary trade.

Prince Henry the Navigator of Portugal organizing an expedition to sail down the west coast of Africa. At first the sailors hoped to gain control of the African gold trade from the Muslim merchants, and they built trading posts along the coast. They exchanged horses, cloth, and brassware for gold dust, ivory, and slaves. Then they decided to sail south around Africa to India where they could buy spices. By the time Henry died, ships had reached as far south as the coast of Sierra Leone, and he had started a school of navigation in Portugal.

Vasco da Gama left Lisbon in Portugal on July 8, 1497 to sail to the East. He rounded the tip of Africa, the Cape of Good Hope, and sailed northward. Soon he reached an area where there were many Arab boats sailing from the east coast of Africa to India, and he collected an Arab pilot to show him the way. He sailed across the Indian Ocean to Calicut on the Indian coast. There he collected a cargo of spices and precious stones. His cargo was worth 60 times the cost of his expedition, but three-fourths of his crew died from disease on the voyage.

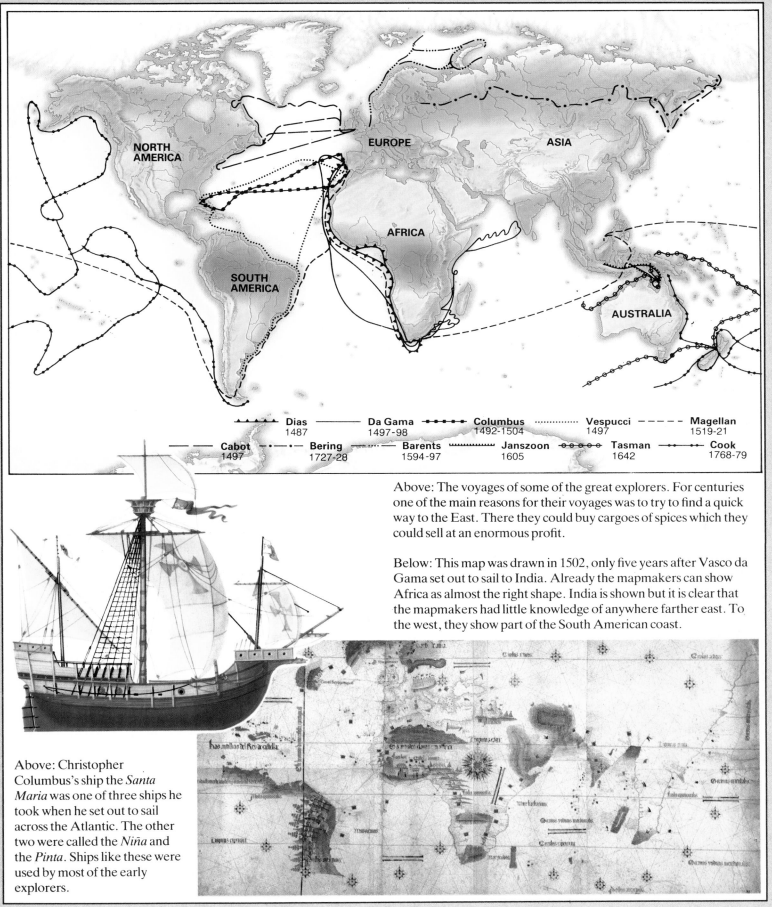

| | | | | |
|---|---|---|---|---|
| ▲▲▲▲ **Dias** 1487 | ———— **Da Gama** 1497-98 | •–•–•– **Columbus** 1492-1504 | ·········· **Vespucci** 1497 | — — — **Magellan** 1519-21 |
| —•— **Cabot** 1497 | —•—•— **Bering** 1727-28 | ～～～～ **Barents** 1594-97 | ～～～～ **Janszoon** 1605 | ◦◦◦◦ **Tasman** 1642 | •◦•◦ **Cook** 1768-79 |

Above: The voyages of some of the great explorers. For centuries one of the main reasons for their voyages was to try to find a quick way to the East. There they could buy cargoes of spices which they could sell at an enormous profit.

Below: This map was drawn in 1502, only five years after Vasco da Gama set out to sail to India. Already the mapmakers can show Africa as almost the right shape. India is shown but it is clear that the mapmakers had little knowledge of anywhere farther east. To the west, they show part of the South American coast.

Above: Christopher Columbus's ship the *Santa Maria* was one of three ships he took when he set out to sail across the Atlantic. The other two were called the *Niña* and the *Pinta*. Ships like these were used by most of the early explorers.

# The New World

Christopher Columbus reached America in 1492. Within a few years many other Europeans, eager to make their fortunes, arrived in the New World, as they called North and South America and the West Indies.

The Spaniards flocked to Mexico and Peru. The Aztecs and the Incas did not stand a chance against the Spaniards with their horses, armor, steel swords, and guns. By the middle 1500s the Spaniards had wiped out the great empires. They made slaves of the people and forced them to become Christians. Untold numbers of Indians died from European diseases, or from cruelty.

Farmers also went to the New World. They grew the local crops but they also took with them European plants and animals. Those settling in Central and South America were Spaniards and Portuguese. Farther north were English, French, and Dutch settlers. Among the earliest settlers in North America were the Pilgrim Fathers who sailed from England in 1620. They were soon followed by others. A number of French people went to what is now Canada. Then they explored south, along the rivers that lay west of the English and Dutch settlements. They claimed Louisiana, along the Mississippi River, for France.

As more and more European settlers arrived, looking for land to farm, the Indians were in the way. There were battles. The Indians here, as in South America, died in large numbers. Gradually the east coast colonies were cleared of Indians.

In the colonies two different ways of life gradually grew up. In the northern states, people mostly worked their own small farms, or were trappers or traders. But farther south, people owned much larger estates. On their plantations they grew one main crop such as sugar, cotton, or tobacco. They made slaves, bought or captured in West Africa, work for them. Over 10 million slaves were taken to the Americas before the trade was stopped in the 1800s.

Above: This painting of an Indian village, Pomeioc, dates from about 1585. It is one of several done by an Englishman called John White, who led an expedition to found a colony on the island of Roanoke, in what is now North Carolina. It failed because it included too many adventurers hoping to find gold, and too few genuine settlers. The first successful English settlement was in 1607.

Left: This map of about 1540 shows the French explorer Jacques Cartier and his men in Canada, Cartier was sent by the French King Francis I to look for a way of sailing north-west around America to reach the East. He never discovered such a route, but as he searched for it he discovered the St. Lawrence River.

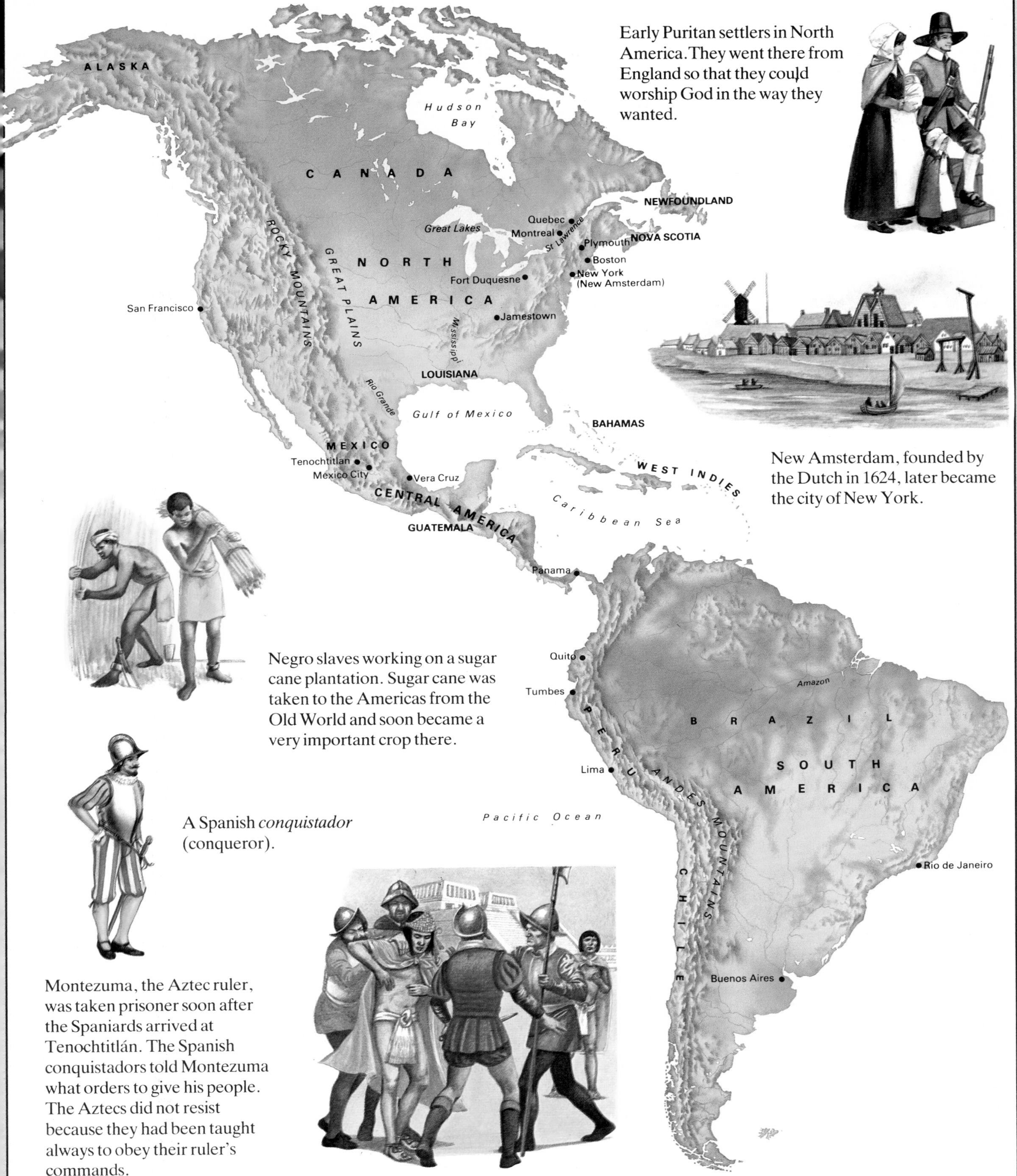
ALASKA
Hudson Bay
CANADA
NEWFOUNDLAND
Quebec
Montreal
St Lawrence
Great Lakes
Plymouth
NOVA SCOTIA
Boston
ROCKY MOUNTAINS
GREAT PLAINS
NORTH AMERICA
Fort Duquesne
New York
(New Amsterdam)
San Francisco
Jamestown
Mississippi
LOUISIANA
Rio Grande
Gulf of Mexico
BAHAMAS
MEXICO
Tenochtitlan
Mexico City
Vera Cruz
WEST INDIES
CENTRAL AMERICA
GUATEMALA
Caribbean Sea
Panama
Quito
Tumbes
Amazon
BRAZIL
PERU
ANDES MOUNTAINS
Lima
SOUTH AMERICA
Pacific Ocean
Rio de Janeiro
CHILE
Buenos Aires

Early Puritan settlers in North America. They went there from England so that they could worship God in the way they wanted.

New Amsterdam, founded by the Dutch in 1624, later became the city of New York.

Negro slaves working on a sugar cane plantation. Sugar cane was taken to the Americas from the Old World and soon became a very important crop there.

A Spanish *conquistador* (conqueror).

Montezuma, the Aztec ruler, was taken prisoner soon after the Spaniards arrived at Tenochtitlán. The Spanish conquistadors told Montezuma what orders to give his people. The Aztecs did not resist because they had been taught always to obey their ruler's commands.

# Renaissance and Reformation

In the 1400s Italian artists and scholars became fascinated by the arts and learning of Ancient Greece and Rome. This time became known as the *Renaissance*, which means "revival" or "rebirth." Painters and sculptors studied ancient art and then tried to make their own pictures and statues lifelike. Instead of showing only religious subjects, they began to produce works showing scenes from history and important recent events. Architects copied the proportions and pillars of Greek buildings and the domes and arches of Roman buildings to make a new style of their own.

For a long time learning had been controlled by the Church. Now scholars studied Latin, Greek, and Hebrew. People became interested in the world around them. Some of their findings got them into trouble with the Church, because they went against what people then believed to be true.

The new interest in art and learning spread across Europe. It was helped by the invention of printing in the 1450s.

The wish to talk over problems and look for ways of solving them spilt over into Church matters. By the 1500s many people were unhappy with the way the Church was being run. This led to a movement called the "Reformation" to change and reform the Church.

One man who hoped to reform the Church was a German monk, Martin Luther. Many people resented his criticisms and attacked his ideas, but he had a great deal of support.

The people who followed Luther and protested that changes were needed were known as Protestants. Those who remained faithful to the old Church, headed by the pope in Rome, were the Roman Catholics. Soon Protestant groups grew up in many parts of Europe. Meanwhile, the leaders of the Catholic Church called a great council at Trent in Italy to work out how they could make their Church better. Wars broke out over religion not just inside countries, but between countries too. These included the Thirty Years' War, from 1618 to 1648.

### Martin Luther

In 1517, a German monk, Martin Luther, nailed a list of 95 "theses" (complaints) about the Church to the door of Wittenberg Church in Germany. Luther set up his own organization of Christians in Germany. He and his followers became known as Protestants because they protested against some of the ways and beliefs of the Roman Catholic Church.

The Italian Renaissance painter, Botticelli's *Primavera* (Spring), painted in about 1477. This detail of the Three Graces shows the influence of the classical Greek and Roman art on Renaissance art.

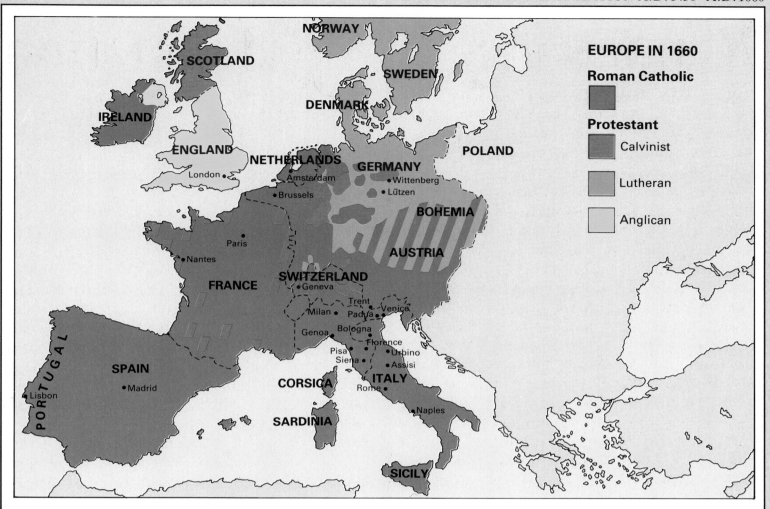

EUROPE IN 1660

**Roman Catholic**

**Protestant**
Calvinist
Lutheran
Anglican

Above: This map shows Roman Catholic and Protestant parts of Europe in 1660. The cream-colored area on the right was mixed. At first the Protestants gained enormous numbers of supporters all over northern Europe and France, but by now the Catholic Church had won many people back. It remained a single body, but the Protestants were split up into different groups.

Below: The city of Florence in Italy was one of the great centers of art and learning in the Renaissance. Most of the famous people of the time lived and worked in Florence. This view shows the cathedral dome built in the early 1400s by Brunelleschi. Architects built beautiful palaces and churches and they copied the style of the Ancient Greek and Roman temples.

# The Pacific

Captain Cook visited Tahiti where he was met by war canoes on his first voyage to the Pacific in 1768.

Dutch sailors blown west from the tip of South Africa discovered the north and west coasts of Australia by accident in the 1600s. Later that century Abel Tasman sailed right around Australia without realizing it was there, although he landed on the island called Tasmania after him. When he reached New Zealand he believed he had found part of a huge mass of land which became known as *Terra Australis Incognita*, the Latin for "the unknown land to the south."

In 1768 an English sailor, James Cook, was sent to look for this great southern land. He sailed to New Zealand, which he claimed for Britain and then on to the east coast of Australia. Cook claimed much of eastern Australia for Britain. He called it New South Wales. In 1788 the first British settlers arrived there. They were convicts and their guards. Soon free settlers arrived to farm the land. Then gold was discovered. In the 1850s people rushed to Australia from all over the world, hoping to find gold and make their fortunes. By the end of the 1800s there were a number of different British colonies in Australia. In 1901 they became states and joined together to make up the Commonwealth of Australia.

Cook was the first European to land in New Zealand. Tasman had tried to land more than a hundred years before, but had been driven off by the Maori people who lived there. The first settlers from Britain did not arrive until 1840. They began to farm the rich country, buying land from the Maoris. This led to quarrels and there was war between the Maoris and the white settlers, but peace was made in 1870.

Cook's voyages across the Pacific opened up the area to Europeans. Missionaries converted the islanders to Christianity and taught them European ways, while traders grew rich from the products they sent home.

## Captain Cook

Between 1768 and 1779 Captain Cook, the English explorer, led three long expeditions to the Pacific Ocean. He was a great mapmaker and navigator. He made very accurate maps and took great care to make detailed notes on his travels. From his voyages he showed that there was no great land mass, but instead the huge island of Australia. On a fateful voyage in 1779 he was killed in a quarrel with the people of Hawaii. But he left behind him a wealth of information and paved the way for settlement in Australia and New Zealand. His ship *Endeavour* (left) was little bigger than the ships of the great Portuguese explorers but he had better instruments to help him find out exactly where he was.

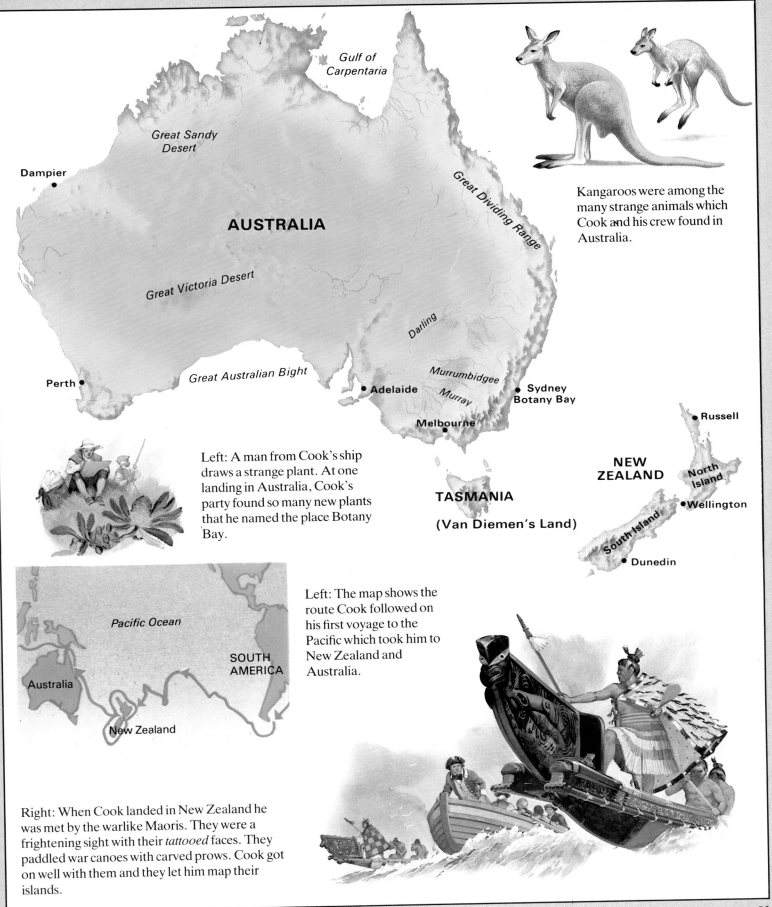

Gulf of Carpentaria

Great Sandy Desert

Dampier

Great Dividing Range

AUSTRALIA

Great Victoria Desert

Darling

Perth

Great Australian Bight

Murrumbidgee

Adelaide

Murray

Sydney
Botany Bay

Melbourne

Kangaroos were among the many strange animals which Cook and his crew found in Australia.

Russell

NEW ZEALAND

North Island

TASMANIA

(Van Diemen's Land)

Wellington

South Island

Dunedin

Left: A man from Cook's ship draws a strange plant. At one landing in Australia, Cook's party found so many new plants that he named the place Botany Bay.

Pacific Ocean

SOUTH AMERICA

Australia

New Zealand

Left: The map shows the route Cook followed on his first voyage to the Pacific which took him to New Zealand and Australia.

Right: When Cook landed in New Zealand he was met by the warlike Maoris. They were a frightening sight with their *tattooed* faces. They paddled war canoes with carved prows. Cook got on well with them and they let him map their islands.

# The Empire Builders

The great empires of the past grew powerful and gained control of their neighbors. During the 1700s a different sort of empire was growing up, as Europeans spread out all over the world. These new empires were scattered over far distant continents, often many weeks' journeys from their mother countries.

The first Europeans to reach Central and South America soon conquered the people living there. The Indians of North America fought fiercely for hundreds of years, but eventually the Europeans controlled the whole country. In Australia and New Zealand, too, the British took the countries over. Today these countries are independent. But most of the people there are descended wholly or partly from Europeans.

The first Europeans to arrive in the East were the Portuguese. They came to trade and not to build an empire, but soon they decided to take control of the "spice route" along which their ships sailed. Meanwhile the Spanish took over the Philippines. Before long the Dutch, English, and then the French sailed onto the scene. They set up East India companies to organize trading and settlements. The Dutch, who had better ships,

drove the Portuguese from the Spice Islands. To safeguard their trade, the Europeans employed soldiers and made treaties with the local rulers. A number of treaties with local rulers gave the British control over most of India.

When these countries became independent again, most of the Europeans went home. They left behind a framework of government and communications and of western skills, which the new countries could use if they wished to.

Above: This bridge is typically Dutch, but it is in Djakarta, on the island of Java in Indonesia. The Dutch ruled these islands for several hundred years.

Left: Soldiers of the Indian Army in 1902. India was divided into provinces, each ruled by a British governor, and states, ruled by Indian princes. They let the British manage their foreign affairs in return for military protection. In 1878 Queen Victoria was made Empress of India, and she took a great interest in the country. The Indian Army included British and Indian officers and Indian soldiers.

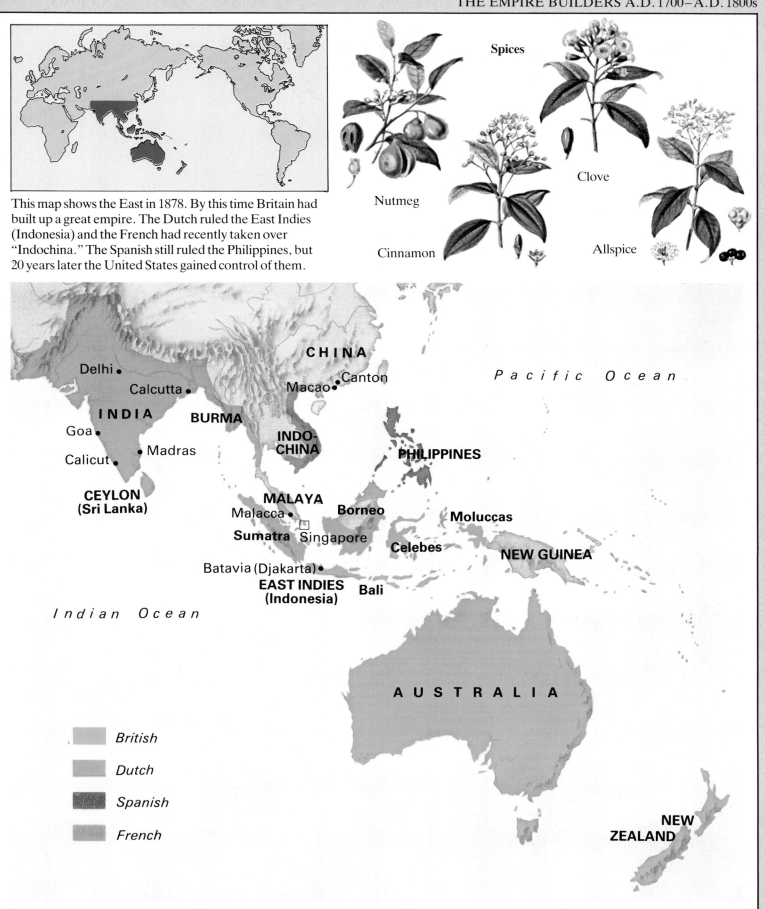

**Spices**

Nutmeg

Cinnamon

Clove

Allspice

This map shows the East in 1878. By this time Britain had built up a great empire. The Dutch ruled the East Indies (Indonesia) and the French had recently taken over "Indochina." The Spanish still ruled the Philippines, but 20 years later the United States gained control of them.

*Pacific Ocean*

CHINA

Delhi

Calcutta

Macao • Canton

INDIA

BURMA

Goa

Calicut • Madras

INDO-CHINA

PHILIPPINES

CEYLON
(Sri Lanka)

MALAYA

Malacca •

Borneo

Moluccas

Sumatra • Singapore

Celebes

NEW GUINEA

Batavia (Djakarta) •

EAST INDIES
(Indonesia)

Bali

*Indian Ocean*

British

Dutch

Spanish

French

A U S T R A L I A

NEW
ZEALAND

# Across the World

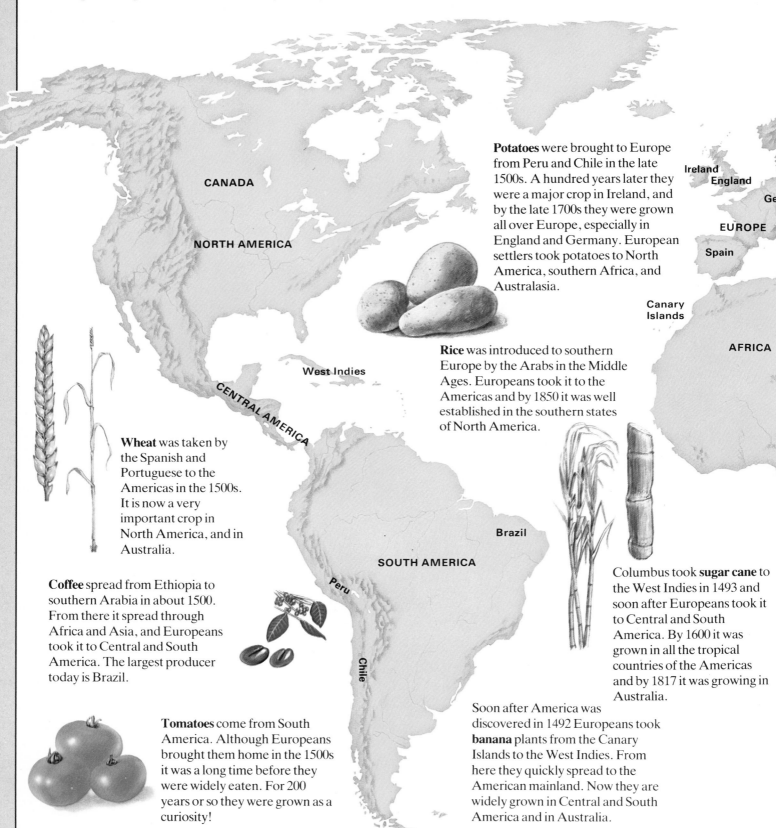

CANADA

NORTH AMERICA

**Potatoes** were brought to Europe from Peru and Chile in the late 1500s. A hundred years later they were a major crop in Ireland, and by the late 1700s they were grown all over Europe, especially in England and Germany. European settlers took potatoes to North America, southern Africa, and Australasia.

Ireland
England
Ger
EUROPE
Spain
Canary Islands
AFRICA

**Rice** was introduced to southern Europe by the Arabs in the Middle Ages. Europeans took it to the Americas and by 1850 it was well established in the southern states of North America.

West Indies

CENTRAL AMERICA

**Wheat** was taken by the Spanish and Portuguese to the Americas in the 1500s. It is now a very important crop in North America, and in Australia.

Brazil

SOUTH AMERICA

Peru

Chile

**Coffee** spread from Ethiopia to southern Arabia in about 1500. From there it spread through Africa and Asia, and Europeans took it to Central and South America. The largest producer today is Brazil.

Columbus took **sugar cane** to the West Indies in 1493 and soon after Europeans took it to Central and South America. By 1600 it was grown in all the tropical countries of the Americas and by 1817 it was growing in Australia.

**Tomatoes** come from South America. Although Europeans brought them home in the 1500s it was a long time before they were widely eaten. For 200 years or so they were grown as a curiosity!

Soon after America was discovered in 1492 Europeans took **banana** plants from the Canary Islands to the West Indies. From here they quickly spread to the American mainland. Now they are widely grown in Central and South America and in Australia.

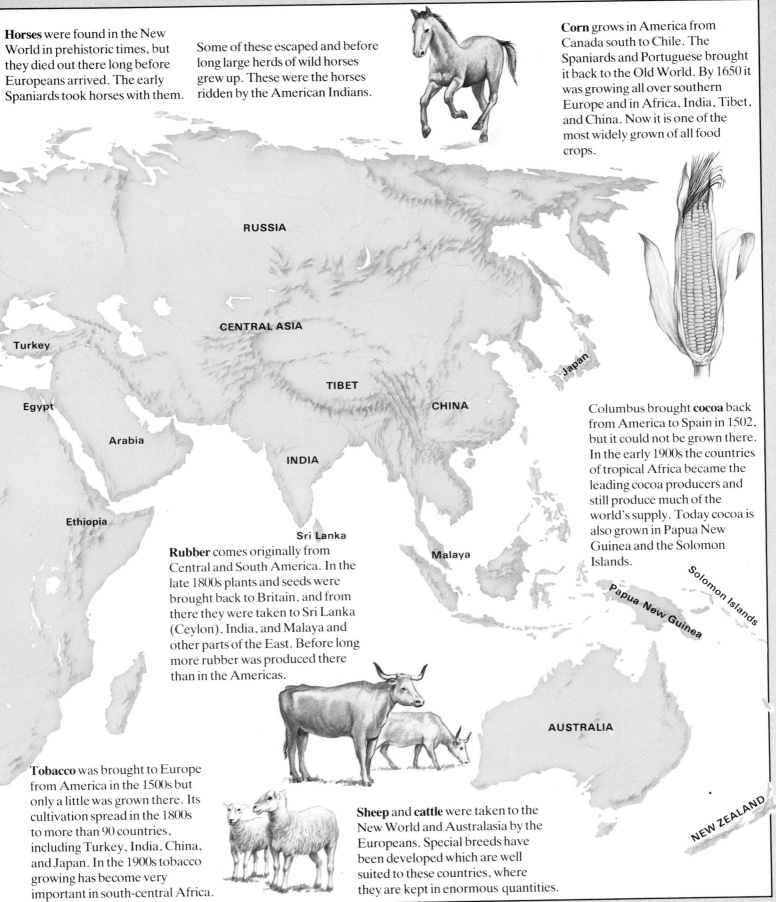

**Horses** were found in the New World in prehistoric times, but they died out there long before Europeans arrived. The early Spaniards took horses with them.

Some of these escaped and before long large herds of wild horses grew up. These were the horses ridden by the American Indians.

**Corn** grows in America from Canada south to Chile. The Spaniards and Portuguese brought it back to the Old World. By 1650 it was growing all over southern Europe and in Africa, India, Tibet, and China. Now it is one of the most widely grown of all food crops.

RUSSIA

CENTRAL ASIA

Turkey

Egypt

Arabia

TIBET

CHINA

Japan

INDIA

Ethiopia

Sri Lanka

Malaya

Columbus brought **cocoa** back from America to Spain in 1502, but it could not be grown there. In the early 1900s the countries of tropical Africa became the leading cocoa producers and still produce much of the world's supply. Today cocoa is also grown in Papua New Guinea and the Solomon Islands.

Solomon Islands

Papua New Guinea

**Rubber** comes originally from Central and South America. In the late 1800s plants and seeds were brought back to Britain, and from there they were taken to Sri Lanka (Ceylon), India, and Malaya and other parts of the East. Before long more rubber was produced there than in the Americas.

AUSTRALIA

NEW ZEALAND

**Tobacco** was brought to Europe from America in the 1500s but only a little was grown there. Its cultivation spread in the 1800s to more than 90 countries, including Turkey, India, China, and Japan. In the 1900s tobacco growing has become very important in south-central Africa.

**Sheep** and **cattle** were taken to the New World and Australasia by the Europeans. Special breeds have been developed which are well suited to these countries, where they are kept in enormous quantities.

57

# THE AGE OF REVOLUTIONS

The 1700s were the start of an age of revolutions. In America and in France the people overturned their old system of government. The success of these revolutions had a great effect on the rest of the world. Many people in Europe and in the Spanish colonies in South America were influenced by the new spirit of freedom. Many countries fought and gained their independence and in the early 1900s the people of Russia rose up and overthrew the Tsar and his government.

Meanwhile another kind of revolution was taking place. The invention of steam engines led to the growth of large industries. This brought many changes in the way in which people lived. By the end of the 1800s events in one country could affect places across the Earth.

## The Americas

● France lost its empire in North America (1). Britain held Canada and the Atlantic coast, while the lands west of the Mississippi belonged to Spain. The Spaniards also moved north from their Latin American colonies, and settled in California (3).

● In 1776 thirteen of Britain's colonies gained independence. War followed until in 1783 the United States of America was recognized. In 1861 civil war broke out between the states of the North and South. It lasted until 1865 when the North won. All slaves were freed.

● Many Spanish colonies in Latin America gained their independence. Bolívar led New Granada (4) to independence from Spain.

● In 1903 the first powered flight was made by the Wright brothers in North Carolina (2).

## Africa

● North Africa (7) remained under Ottoman rule, while European trading stations along the west coast (6) flourished through the slave trade with the Americas.

● In the south, Dutch settlers moved inland from their original settlements on the Cape of Good Hope (5) but in 1899 Britain took over Cape Colony from the Dutch (Boers). In 1910 the Union of South Africa was formed.

● In 1869 the Suez Canal (8) was opened, joining the Mediterranean to the Red Sea.

● In 1884 important European countries laid down rules for their claims on Africa.

## Europe

● The Seven Years' War from 1756 to 1763 between Austria, France, Russia, and Sweden on one side and Britain, Hanover, and Prussia on the other ended with Britain dominant.

● In England (15) in 1733 John Kay produced his "flying shuttle," the first important textile invention, to speed up weaving. In 1804 Richard Trevithick developed the steam locomotive.

## The Near East

● The Ottomans ruled the area (9) but their days of expansion had come to an end. Greece (11) became independent in 1830 and many other countries gained independence under powerful governors.

● In 1854 the Crimean War (10) broke out between Russia and Turkey. The war ended with a Russian defeat in 1856. Disease caused more deaths than fighting, but British hospitals were set up under Florence Nightingale.

**Europe**
- In 1789 the French Revolution broke out (14). In 1792 a republic was set up, and in 1799 Napoleon Bonaparte took power in France. In 1804 he crowned himself Emperor. In a series of wars he gained control of much of Europe. He was defeated by the British and Prussians in 1815 at Waterloo.

- Prussia (13) became a leading military power and in 1871 Germany was united as an empire under the King of Prussia.
- Belgium (17) broke away from the Netherlands (18) in 1830 to become independent.
- In 1837 Queen Victoria came to the throne in Britain (15).

Her reign lasted until 1901.
- In 1846 there was a terrible famine in Ireland (16) because a disease ruined most of the potato crop.
- The Kingdom of Italy (12) was set up in 1861.
- 1914 saw the outbreak of World War I.

**Russia**
- Russia gained land on the Baltic Sea (19) and from Finland (20), Poland (21) and Bessarabia (22).
- In 1904 war broke out with Japan and the Russians were defeated.
- In 1905 a revolution in Russia was stopped when the Tsar made some reforms. But in the 1917 revolution the Tsar was overthrown by the Bolshevik party led by Lenin.

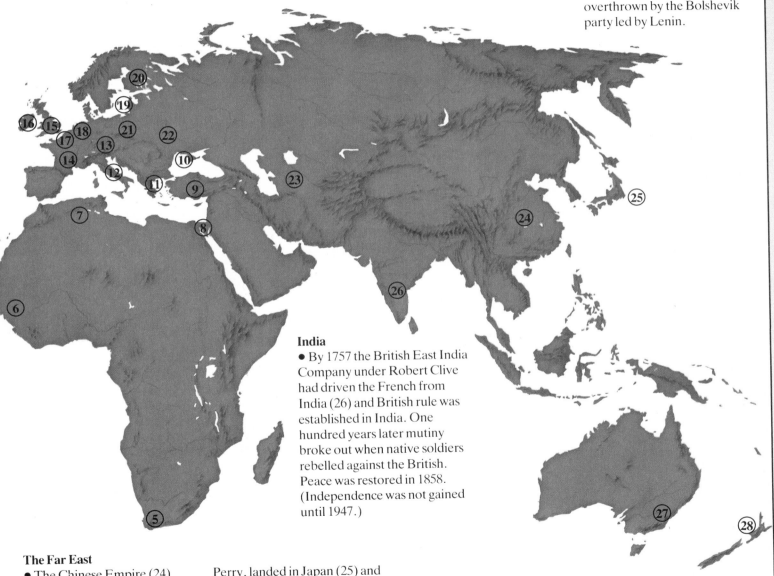

**India**
- By 1757 the British East India Company under Robert Clive had driven the French from India (26) and British rule was established in India. One hundred years later mutiny broke out when native soldiers rebelled against the British. Peace was restored in 1858. (Independence was not gained until 1947.)

**The Far East**
- The Chinese Empire (24) reached its greatest extent with the annexing of Turkestan (23) in 1759.
- China and Japan remained cut off from the rest of the world. But in 1854, a U.S. Naval officer, Commodore

Perry, landed in Japan (25) and forced the Japanese to open their country to foreign trade.
- In 1900 Chinese nationalists (Boxers) attacked Europeans in several Chinese towns but they were defeated by international force.

**Australia and New Zealand**
- In 1788 the first British settlers arrived in Australia (27) and settlements were established with the help of convict labor. (Britain soon claimed all of Australia.)

- British settlers arrived in New Zealand (28) in 1840. Wars were fought with the Maoris, but peace was made in 1870.

# The Industrial Revolution

In the early 1700s farming in Britain changed completely. The change, called the "Agricultural Revolution," later spread to other parts of Europe. New crops were grown and fertilizers were used so better crops were produced. Better animals were bred and inventors made machines to help with hoeing and sowing seeds.

Most people lived and worked in the countryside in the 1700s until the "Industrial Revolution," when major changes occurred in transport and industry. People found out how to turn coal into coke, which could be used to make iron. Iron was used for building bridges, machines, ships, and many other things. By 1800 Britain produced more iron and coal than all the rest of the world together.

In the early 1700s people began to make machines driven by the power of steam. In England, in 1804, Richard Trevithick built the first steam locomotive to run on rails. Twenty years later, the first passenger railway was opened. Travel was now quick and cheap.

Britain was the first country to have an industrial revolution, but soon other countries followed. In the late 1800s came another wave of changes. Steel, made mainly in Germany and the United States, replaced iron. The chemical industry grew up and new sources of power were developed. Many new inventions followed, and people's lives changed more and more.

Left: In the 1800s in Britain new factories employed lots of people. This map shows the towns that grew up around the factories and the main centers of industry.

Below: Women at work in a textile mill in the early 1800s. Until the mid-1700s cloth was made by hand by villagers in their cottages. But with the invention of machines cloth was produced in factories.

Below: New ways of farming brought great wealth to landowners, but villagers who could no longer graze their animals on common land suffered. Many of them went to work in the new towns which grew up around the factories. The houses they lived in there were crowded together and very unhealthy. Working conditions were appalling and men, women and children had to work very long hours.

# Napoleon's Europe

During the 1500s, 1600s, and 1700s Europeans explored the world and built up great empires. At home, most of their countries were ruled by powerful kings or emperors, and ordinary people had little or no say in how things were run. During the 1700s some people began to think that everyone had the right to a say in how they were governed.

In 1789 in France, the poor people were taxed so heavily and had so few rights that they rose up against their rulers. During the French Revolution, as their rebellion is called, their king, Louis XVI, and queen, Marie Antoinette, and many nobles were executed.

Other European rulers were alarmed by events in France and soon the French were at war with the rest of Europe. A general called Napoleon rose to power in France. He raised a huge citizen army, for which all childless men between the ages of 18 and 40 could be called up. With it he gained control of much of Europe and turned several rulers off their thrones. In 1804, he had crowned himself Emperor of the French and ruler of the huge European empire he had conquered. But in 1815, he was defeated at the Battle of Waterloo by the British and Prussians.

Napoleon's empire was freed from French rule and France was once again governed by kings. But people now realized that rulers and frontiers could be changed.

Right: Napoleon Bonaparte. After the turmoil of the French Revolution he took over the rule of France. He died in 1821 in exile on the lonely South Atlantic island of St. Helena.

Above: The map of Europe shows the vast area which Napoleon conquered for France. It also shows his route to Moscow.
Below: Napoleon and his army on their retreat from Moscow. Napoleon was determined to add Russia to his Empire and in June 1812 he invaded it with 600,000 men. He captured Moscow, but as the bitterly cold Russian winter set in he had to retreat. Only 100,000 of his men survived.

61

# Independence in the Americas

In 1776, 13 British colonies in North America declared themselves independent. They fought against their British rulers and set up their own republic of the United States of America. Before long other colonies in the Americas were following their example.

Much of Central and South America was part of a huge Spanish empire over 300 years old. In the early 1800s Simón Bolívar set out to free his country from Spanish rule. He knew that he and his followers could never beat the Spanish troops in battle. Instead Bolívar and his followers, who knew the countryside well, fought *guerilla* war. In a series of wars between 1811 and 1825 they freed northern South America from Spanish rule. Meanwhile, Mexicans rose up to free themselves, and in the south, José de San Martin led the people to drive out the Spaniards.

In 1848 gold was discovered in California. Thousands of people moved there in a great "gold rush." Railroads were built to link east and west, and by 1869 a railway stretched right across the continent. It crossed the Great Plains, lived in by the Indians, who hunted the buffalo which roamed there. The white men soon wiped out the buffalo and fought the Indians. By 1890, the Indians and the buffalo were found only in special reservations. The Plains were settled by farmers, who raised great herds of cattle and planted vast fields of wheat.

All through the 1800s, Europeans were sailing west to America. They settled in the United States, becoming farmers or working in the new industries that were growing up in the east. By 1900 the United States had become an important industrial nation.

Above: The battle of Williamsburg, during the American Civil War. Here the advancing Unionists (northerners—in blue) clashed with the Confederates (southerners). The Confederates withdrew after heavy fighting. The Civil War broke out in 1861 and ended four years later after over 630,000 people had been killed.

Left: Backed up by the French, the American army finally forced the British to surrender at Yorktown, Virginia, in October 1781. The peace treaty was signed in Paris two years later recognizing the United States of America as an independent nation.

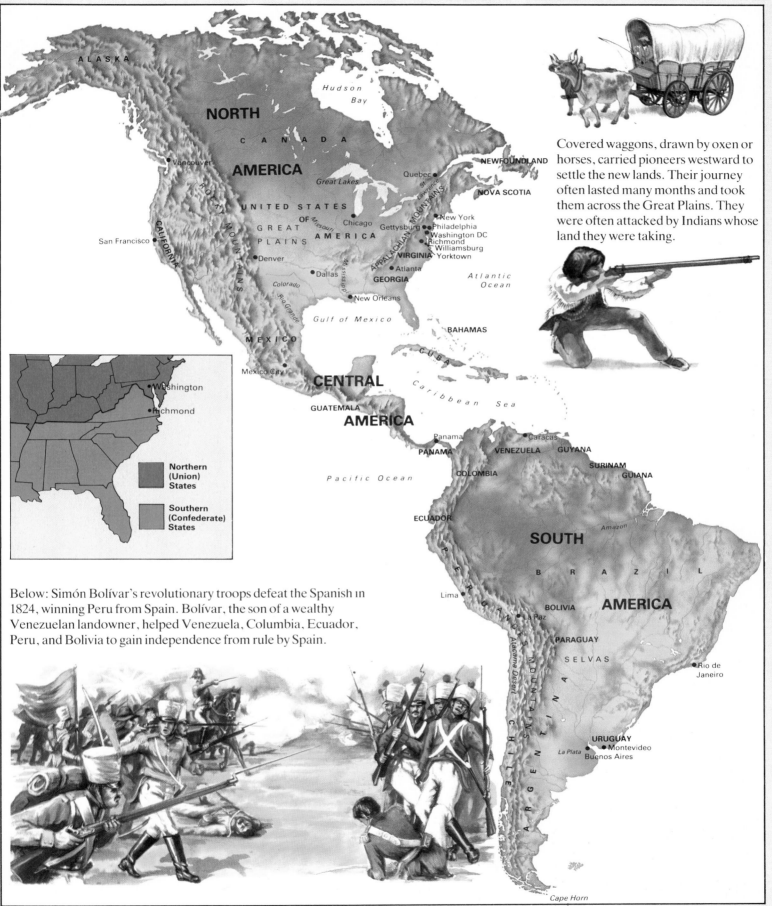

ALASKA

NORTH

C A N A D A

AMERICA

*Hudson Bay*

Vancouver

NEWFOUNDLAND

Quebec

*Great Lakes*

*St. Lawrence*

NOVA SCOTIA

UNITED STATES

*Missouri*

OF

Chicago

New York

Gettysburg

Philadelphia

Washington DC

GREAT

Richmond

AMERICA

Williamsburg

San Francisco

PLAINS

VIRGINIA

Yorktown

CALIFORNIA

ROCKY MOUNTAINS

APPALACHIAN MOUNTAINS

GEORGIA

Denver

Atlanta

*Atlantic Ocean*

*Colorado*

Dallas

*Mississippi*

*Rio Grande*

New Orleans

MEXICO

*Gulf of Mexico*

BAHAMAS

Mexico City

CENTRAL

C U B A

*Caribbean Sea*

GUATEMALA

AMERICA

Panama

Caracas

PANAMA

VENEZUELA

GUYANA

*Pacific Ocean*

COLOMBIA

SURINAM

GUIANA

ECUADOR

SOUTH

*Amazon*

B R A Z I L

AMERICA

Lima

BOLIVIA

La Paz

PERUAN ANDES MOUNTAINS

PARAGUAY

SELVAS

Rio de Janeiro

*Atacama Desert*

ARGENTINA

CHILE

URUGUAY

*La Plata*

Montevideo

Buenos Aires

*Cape Horn*

Covered waggons, drawn by oxen or horses, carried pioneers westward to settle the new lands. Their journey often lasted many months and took them across the Great Plains. They were often attacked by Indians whose land they were taking.

Washington

Richmond

**Northern (Union) States**

**Southern (Confederate) States**

Below: Simón Bolívar's revolutionary troops defeat the Spanish in 1824, winning Peru from Spain. Bolívar, the son of a wealthy Venezuelan landowner, helped Venezuela, Columbia, Ecuador, Peru, and Bolivia to gain independence from rule by Spain.

# New Nations in Europe

At the beginning of the 1800s Britain, France, Spain, Portugal, and Switzerland had almost the same borders as they have today. But elsewhere in Europe things were different. Sprawling across central Europe was the Holy Roman Empire. It was made up of hundreds of little states, which were loosely linked under the leadership of the emperor of Austria. Italy, too, was made up of a number of small states and much of southeast Europe was ruled by the Ottoman Turks. The examples of the Americans and of the French had a deep effect on many people in Europe, and a movement known as "Nationalism" emerged.

In the 1800s the Ottoman Empire grew too weak to keep its subject countries. In 1829 the Greeks broke free from the Ottomans. In 1878 a great congress (meeting) of the important European countries was held in Berlin. They agreed that Serbia, Montenegro, and Romania should be independent. Soon other Balkan countries broke away from Turkey.

The Holy Roman Empire was done away with by Napoleon in 1806. The most powerful of its northern states, Prussia, under Prince Otto von Bismarck, united neighboring states to form a new German empire. The king of Prussia became their *Kaiser*, or emperor. Austria in the south had its own empire, together with Hungary which had long been ruled by the Habsburg emperors of Austria. Meanwhile Italy, which had been divided between Austria, the Pope, and several other rulers, won its way to freedom and unity.

The last of the great frontier changes took place after World War I, which ended in 1918. Europe had taken the shape we know today.

Right: Prince Otto von Bismarck became the chief minister of Prussia in 1862.
Left: In 1860 Garibaldi and his soldiers, known as the "Red Shirts," drove the foreigners out of Italy. In 1861 Italy became an independent nation.
Below: The battle of Navarino (1827) was a key point in the war for Greek independence from Turkey. The British, Russian, and French ships defeated the Turkish-Egyptian fleet in Navarino Bay, in southwest Greece.

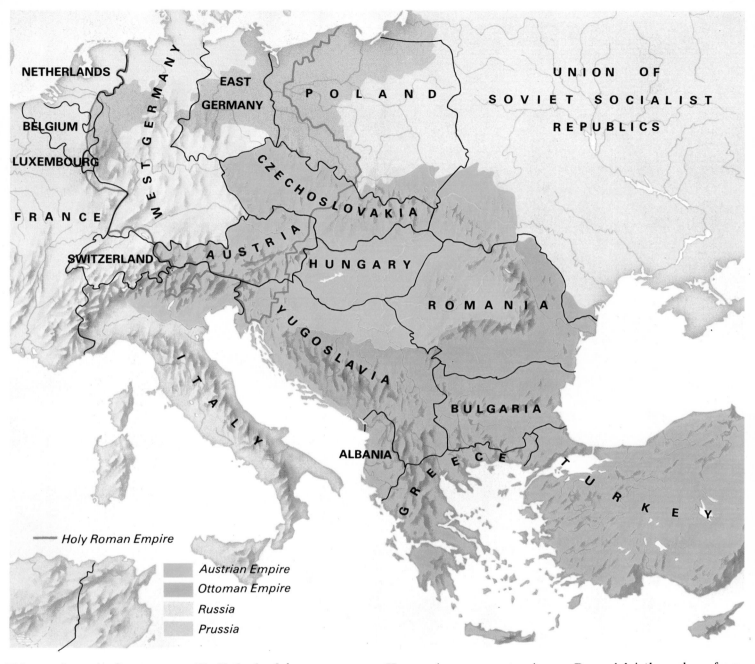

NETHERLANDS

EAST GERMANY

POLAND

UNION OF SOVIET SOCIALIST REPUBLICS

BELGIUM

LUXEMBOURG

WEST GERMANY

CZECHOSLOVAKIA

FRANCE

SWITZERLAND

AUSTRIA

HUNGARY

ROMANIA

ITALY

YUGOSLAVIA

BULGARIA

ALBANIA

GREECE

TURKEY

—— *Holy Roman Empire*

*Austrian Empire*
*Ottoman Empire*
*Russia*
*Prussia*

This map shows the Ottoman Empire, the Austrian Empire, Russia, and Prussia in color, as they were in 1815. The red line shows the old Holy Roman Empire. The borders and names are those of today.

**The Netherlands** became independent from Spain in 1648.

**Belgium,** ruled by Spain, Austria, and then France, was joined to the Netherlands in 1815 but broke away in 1830.

**Czechoslovakia** gained independence in 1918.

**Hungary** became a partner in the Austrian Empire in 1867, and independent in 1918.

**Poland** was divided between Prussia, Austria, and Russia in 1815. It was reunited as an independent country in 1918.

**Yugoslavia** was formed after World War I. Serbia and Montenegro had won freedom from the Ottoman Turks in the 1870s.

**Romania's** independence from the Ottomans was recognized in 1861. After World War I lands from the Austro-Hungarian Empire were joined to it.

**Greece** became an independent kingdom in 1830.

**Bulgaria** became independent in 1908.

**Albania** became independent in 1912.

# Changes in the East

There were two nations in the East which did not become part of any European empire. These were Japan and China. Neither was impressed by what they saw of the first Europeans, and after a little while they closed their countries to them.

But in 1853 the Americans sailed to Japan. Two of the ships were driven by the new steam engines. The Japanese realized that they could not possibly win a sea battle against these powerful ships and agreed to more trading with the West. Then the young Prince Meiji became emperor. He wanted his people to copy the things that made the West powerful.

Japan became strong and it wanted to build up an empire. First it won a war against China. Then it turned against Russia and took over Russian-controlled land on the mainland of China. It then took over Korea and in the 1930s it invaded China. Soon it controlled China's main ports. In World War II the Japanese conquered an enormous empire. Japan was defeated after a few years and lost all its overseas lands. Since the War the Japanese have worked hard and now their country is one of the world's greatest industrial nations.

The Chinese allowed Westerners to trade with them only through the ports of Canton and Macao. They did not like trade with foreigners. The British wanted to extend their trading and so went to war with China in 1839. Britain won and in 1842 forced the Chinese to sign a treaty which gave them Hong Kong and more trading rights.

Little by little, the Chinese learned some Western ways. But many of them felt changes should come more quickly. In 1911 they overthrew the emperor and set up a republic. It began to make changes. Meanwhile, a Communist party was growing up and in 1949 it seized power. Since then, the Chinese people have been working to change centuries-old patterns of life.

Once the Japanese let Europeans into their country, they soon took up Western ideas. This picture shows a group of Japanese people in Western dress. They are playing Western musical instruments. In the 1880s important Japanese people could go to a government-run club to meet foreigners at balls and other events. But in 1888 a new feeling of nationalism swept through Japan. People began to want to keep up the old Japanese ways and went back to wearing their traditional dress. In 1890 the club was closed.

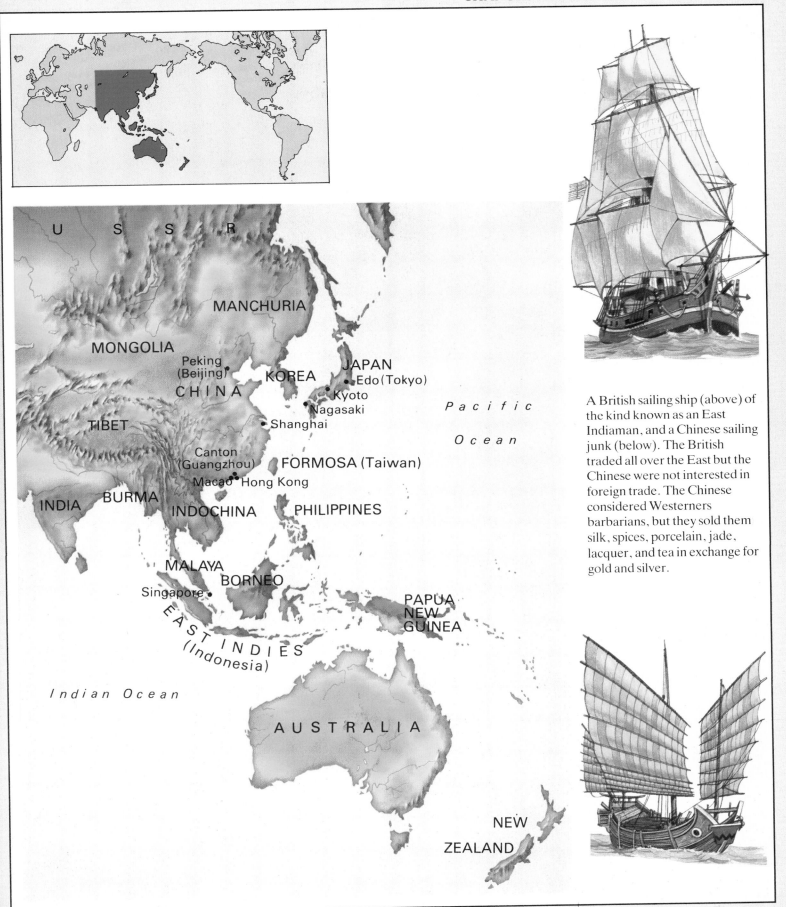

U S S R

MANCHURIA

MONGOLIA

Peking
(Beijing)

KOREA

JAPAN

Edo (Tokyo)

CHINA

Kyoto

Nagasaki

Shanghai

Pacific

Ocean

TIBET

Canton
(Guangzhou)

FORMOSA (Taiwan)

Macao • Hong Kong

INDIA

BURMA

INDOCHINA

PHILIPPINES

MALAYA

BORNEO

Singapore

PAPUA
NEW
GUINEA

E A S T   I N D I E S
(Indonesia)

Indian Ocean

A U S T R A L I A

NEW

ZEALAND

A British sailing ship (above) of
the kind known as an East
Indiaman, and a Chinese sailing
junk (below). The British
traded all over the East but the
Chinese were not interested in
foreign trade. The Chinese
considered Westerners
barbarians, but they sold them
silk, spices, porcelain, jade,
lacquer, and tea in exchange for
gold and silver.

# New Communications

In ancient times people **traveled on foot**, with their goods loaded on pack animals such as camels, asses, and horses. They covered about 3 miles an hour.

A **stage coach** could travel at about 9 miles an hour along reasonable roads.

The **Panama Canal** was opened in 1914. Now people no longer had to sail around South America to travel from the Atlantic Ocean to the Pacific Ocean.

The first non-stop **flight** across the Atlantic was made in 1919 by Alcock and Brown. It took them 16 hours 27 minutes to fly from Newfoundland to Ireland.

Above: The *Spirit of St. Louis*, in which Charles Lindbergh made the first solo transatlantic flight in 1927. Below: The The supersonic *Concorde*.

**Crossing the United States.** In the 1860s the journey by stage coach from St. Joseph in Missouri to Sacramento in California, a distance of 2,000 miles took three weeks. Even the "Pony Express" mail took 10 days. By 1900 a train from New York to Los Angeles, nearly twice as far, took four days. Today the same journey takes under 4 hours by air.

The first **railway** on which all trains were drawn by steam engines was opened in 1830. It ran between Liverpool and Manchester in northern England. A train could travel along it at over 35 miles an hour. Today passenger trains travel at over 120 miles an hour.

Sacramento
NORTH AMERICA
Los Angeles
St Joseph
New York
Mississippi
PACIFIC OCEAN
CENTRAL AMERICA
ATLANTIC OCEAN
Panama Canal
Amazon
SOUTH AMERICA

The **Romans** built good **roads** all over their Empire, from Britain to the river Euphrates. Roman soldiers marched 30 miles in a day, for days at a time, carrying their equipment.

The **Trans-Siberian Railway** links Moscow and Vladivostok. Work on it began in 1891. It covers just under 6,000 miles and the journey takes eight days.

In 1838 the **steamship** *Great Western* sailed from Bristol to New York in 15½ days. A hundred years later, the *Queen Mary*, a huge and luxurious passenger **liner**, made the Atlantic crossing in just under four days, at an average speed of 31.9 knots. Today the journey from London to New York takes three hours by supersonic **plane.**

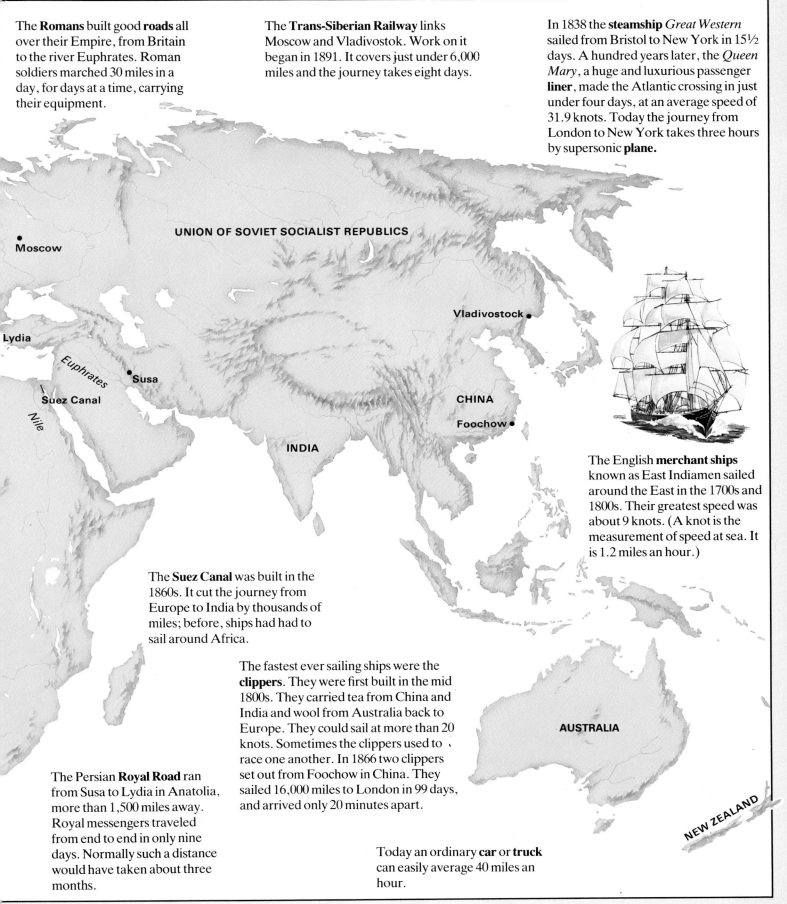

UNION OF SOVIET SOCIALIST REPUBLICS

Moscow

Lydia

Euphrates

Suez Canal

Susa

Nile

Vladivostock

CHINA

Foochow

INDIA

The English **merchant ships** known as East Indiamen sailed around the East in the 1700s and 1800s. Their greatest speed was about 9 knots. (A knot is the measurement of speed at sea. It is 1.2 miles an hour.)

The **Suez Canal** was built in the 1860s. It cut the journey from Europe to India by thousands of miles; before, ships had had to sail around Africa.

The fastest ever sailing ships were the **clippers**. They were first built in the mid 1800s. They carried tea from China and India and wool from Australia back to Europe. They could sail at more than 20 knots. Sometimes the clippers used to race one another. In 1866 two clippers set out from Foochow in China. They sailed 16,000 miles to London in 99 days, and arrived only 20 minutes apart.

AUSTRALIA

The Persian **Royal Road** ran from Susa to Lydia in Anatolia, more than 1,500 miles away. Royal messengers traveled from end to end in only nine days. Normally such a distance would have taken about three months.

Today an ordinary **car** or **truck** can easily average 40 miles an hour.

NEW ZEALAND

# Africa

North Africa became part of the Muslim Empire in the early Middle Ages. Arab traders traveled south across the Sahara Desert to the great medieval kingdoms of Ancient Ghana and Mali, and later to the Songhai Empire on the river Niger. But we know little about the rest of Africa before the Europeans arrived there. The Africans did not develop a written language, so there are no records of their history.

The first Europeans to settle in Africa were the Portuguese. In the 1400s and 1500s they built trading posts on the west coast and at Mozambique on the east coast. They were followed by the Dutch, who founded a colony at the Cape of Good Hope. Portuguese, Dutch, British, and French all took part in the terrible slave trade from the west coast (see page 48).

In 1788 the Association for Promoting the Discovery of the Interior Parts of Africa was set up in London. It began to send expeditions to explore the continent. Many of the first explorers died of fever and some of them disappeared. But by the 1870s the great rivers of Africa had been explored. European countries decided to set up colonies there and they divided the continent between themselves (see opposite page).

Above: This bronze group was made in the forest kingdom of Benin, in West Africa. It shows a king, or *oba*, and two attendants.

The European rule of Africa lasted less than a hundred years. After World War II, almost all the countries became independent. In the south of the continent one white-ruled country remains. This is South Africa, which grew up from the first Dutch settlement. The white people there refuse to share government with the Africans.

Left: Dr. Livingstone arrives at Lake Ngami in 1849. Livingstone went to Africa as a missionary. During his travels he explored the rivers Zambezi and Congo and discovered the Victoria Falls and Lake Nyasa.

Below: The last British colony in Africa to become independent was Zimbabwe, formerly Rhodesia, in 1980. Here British and African leaders sign their agreement.

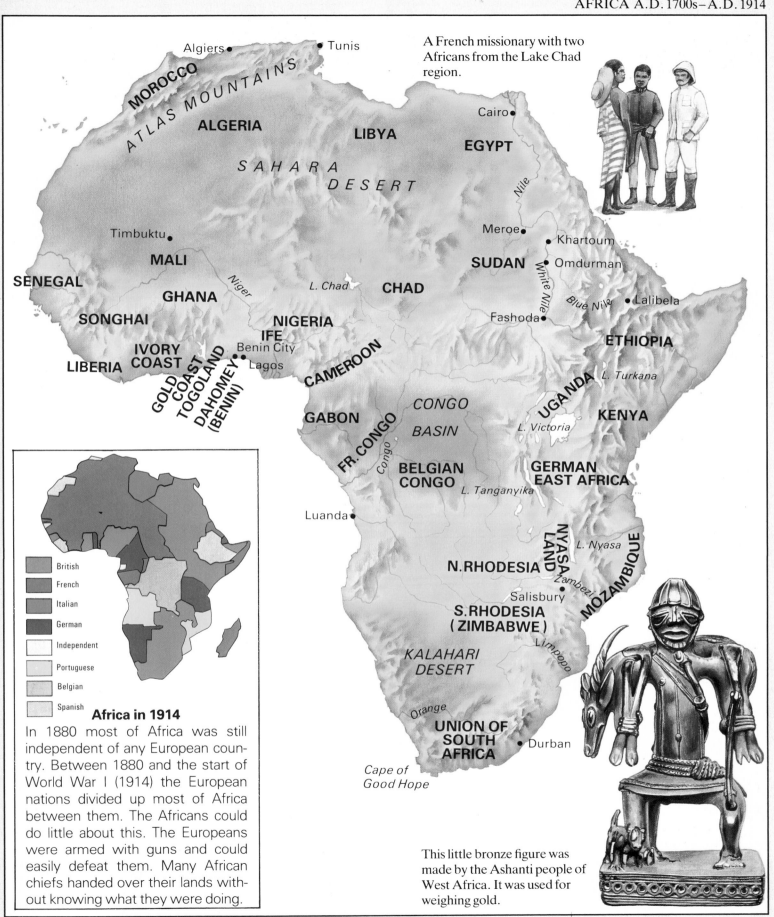

A French missionary with two Africans from the Lake Chad region.

Algiers •     • Tunis

MOROCCO

ATLAS MOUNTAINS

ALGERIA    LIBYA    EGYPT

Cairo •

SAHARA DESERT

Nile

Timbuktu •    Meroe •

MALI    • Khartoum

SUDAN    • Omdurman

SENEGAL    GHANA    L. Chad   CHAD

White Nile

SONGHAI    Niger    Blue Nile    • Lalibela

Fashoda •

IVORY COAST    NIGERIA    IFE

LIBERIA    Benin City    ETHIOPIA

GOLD COAST   TOGOLAND   DAHOMEY (BENIN)    Lagos •    CAMEROON

L. Turkana

UGANDA    KENYA

GABON    CONGO BASIN

FR. CONGO    L. Victoria

Congo

BELGIAN CONGO    GERMAN EAST AFRICA

Luanda •    L. Tanganyika

NYASALAND    L. Nyasa

N. RHODESIA    MOZAMBIQUE

Zambezi

Salisbury •

S. RHODESIA (ZIMBABWE)

KALAHARI DESERT    Limpopo

Orange

UNION OF SOUTH AFRICA    • Durban

Cape of Good Hope

British
French
Italian
German
Independent
Portuguese
Belgian
Spanish

## Africa in 1914

In 1880 most of Africa was still independent of any European country. Between 1880 and the start of World War I (1914) the European nations divided up most of Africa between them. The Africans could do little about this. The Europeans were armed with guns and could easily defeat them. Many African chiefs handed over their lands without knowing what they were doing.

This little bronze figure was made by the Ashanti people of West Africa. It was used for weighing gold.

# THE MODERN WORLD

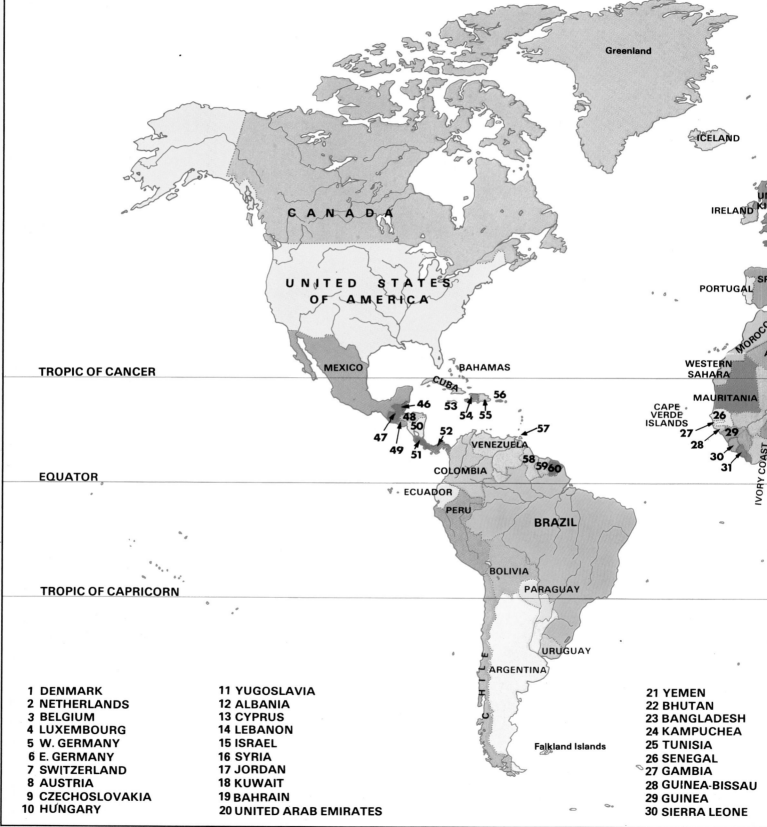

Greenland

ICELAND

IRELAND

UN
KIN

SPA

PORTUGAL

MOROCCO

CANADA

UNITED STATES
OF AMERICA

A

WESTERN
SAHARA

TROPIC OF CANCER

MEXICO

BAHAMAS

CUBA

MAURITANIA

M

CAPE
VERDE
ISLANDS

26

46

53

56

48
50

54 55

27
29

57

52

28

47

49

VENEZUELA

58 5960

30
31

IVORY COAST

51

COLOMBIA

EQUATOR

ECUADOR

PERU

BRAZIL

BOLIVIA

PARAGUAY

TROPIC OF CAPRICORN

URUGUAY

CHILE

ARGENTINA

Falkland Islands

| | | |
|---|---|---|
| 1 DENMARK | 11 YUGOSLAVIA | 21 YEMEN |
| 2 NETHERLANDS | 12 ALBANIA | 22 BHUTAN |
| 3 BELGIUM | 13 CYPRUS | 23 BANGLADESH |
| 4 LUXEMBOURG | 14 LEBANON | 24 KAMPUCHEA |
| 5 W. GERMANY | 15 ISRAEL | 25 TUNISIA |
| 6 E. GERMANY | 16 SYRIA | 26 SENEGAL |
| 7 SWITZERLAND | 17 JORDAN | 27 GAMBIA |
| 8 AUSTRIA | 18 KUWAIT | 28 GUINEA-BISSAU |
| 9 CZECHOSLOVAKIA | 19 BAHRAIN | 29 GUINEA |
| 10 HUNGARY | 20 UNITED ARAB EMIRATES | 30 SIERRA LEONE |

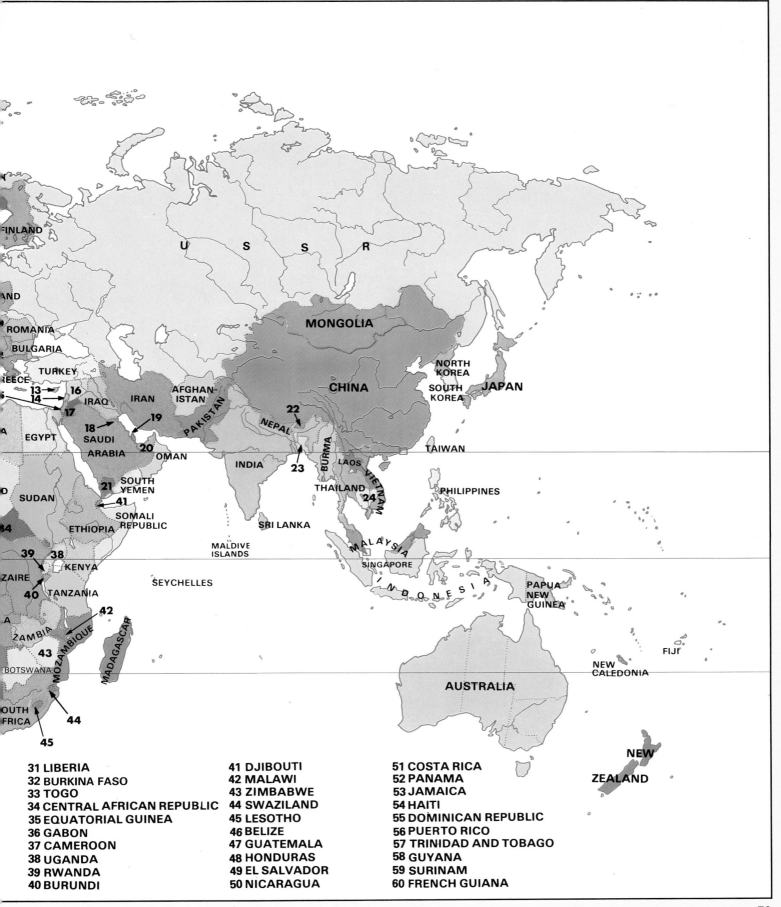

FINLAND

ROMANIA

BULGARIA

TURKEY

GREECE

U S S R

MONGOLIA

13 → 16
14 →
17
IRAQ    IRAN    AFGHAN-ISTAN
PAKISTAN

22

CHINA

NORTH KOREA
SOUTH KOREA
JAPAN

EGYPT

18 →
SAUDI ARABIA
20    OMAN
19

NEPAL

23

BURMA

TAIWAN

LAOS

VIETNAM

21    SOUTH YEMEN

INDIA

THAILAND

24

PHILIPPINES

SUDAN    41
ETHIOPIA    SOMALI REPUBLIC

SRI LANKA

MALDIVE ISLANDS

39    38
ZAIRE    KENYA

40    TANZANIA

SEYCHELLES

MALAYSIA
SINGAPORE

INDONESIA

PAPUA NEW GUINEA

42

ZAMBIA    MOZAMBIQUE    MADAGASCAR

43

BOTSWANA

FIJI

NEW CALEDONIA

AUSTRALIA

SOUTH AFRICA    44

45

NEW ZEALAND

| | | |
|---|---|---|
| 31 LIBERIA | 41 DJIBOUTI | 51 COSTA RICA |
| 32 BURKINA FASO | 42 MALAWI | 52 PANAMA |
| 33 TOGO | 43 ZIMBABWE | 53 JAMAICA |
| 34 CENTRAL AFRICAN REPUBLIC | 44 SWAZILAND | 54 HAITI |
| 35 EQUATORIAL GUINEA | 45 LESOTHO | 55 DOMINICAN REPUBLIC |
| 36 GABON | 46 BELIZE | 56 PUERTO RICO |
| 37 CAMEROON | 47 GUATEMALA | 57 TRINIDAD AND TOBAGO |
| 38 UGANDA | 48 HONDURAS | 58 GUYANA |
| 39 RWANDA | 49 EL SALVADOR | 59 SURINAM |
| 40 BURUNDI | 50 NICARAGUA | 60 FRENCH GUIANA |

# The World at War

This century has seen a number of terrible wars. Two of them are known as world wars, others have been smaller.

World War I (1914–18) was caused by rivalries between nations in Europe, who feared that one country might get too powerful. They made alliances with one another, so that when one country was threatened, others were drawn in to defend it. By the end of the war tanks and planes were coming into use, so when World War II (1939–45) came, it was fought in a different way. Now Britain, France, Russia, and their allies were fighting to prevent the Nazi Germans and Fascist Italians controlling Europe. This war spread to the Pacific when the Japanese attacked the U.S. and invaded British, French, and Dutch colonies.

In World War II the Russians fought on the side of the British and Americans. But after the war, their alliance broke up. The USSR (Russia) set up Communist governments in the countries of eastern Europe. A rivalry developed between the Americans and the Russians known as the "Cold War." It is not a war in the true sense, since they have not fought each other. Both have built up groups of allies (see map opposite).

After World War II the Communists took over power in China and several other Asian countries. The Americans tried to stop Communism spreading. They and their allies prevented the Communists in North Korea from taking over South Korea. Later the Americans fought a bitter war against Communism in Vietnam, but they withdrew and Vietnam and its neighbors are now under Communist rule.

At the end of World War II the Americans dropped a new and terrible kind of bomb on Hiroshima in Japan. This was the first nuclear bomb, and it was far more destructive than any bomb known before. Since then, some countries have armed themselves with nuclear bombs. But they know that if one country drops such a bomb others will follow, and many millions of people will be killed.

Vietnamese refugees run for a helicopter to take them to safety. This century has seen millions of people made homeless by wars, and forced to move from the country where they were born.

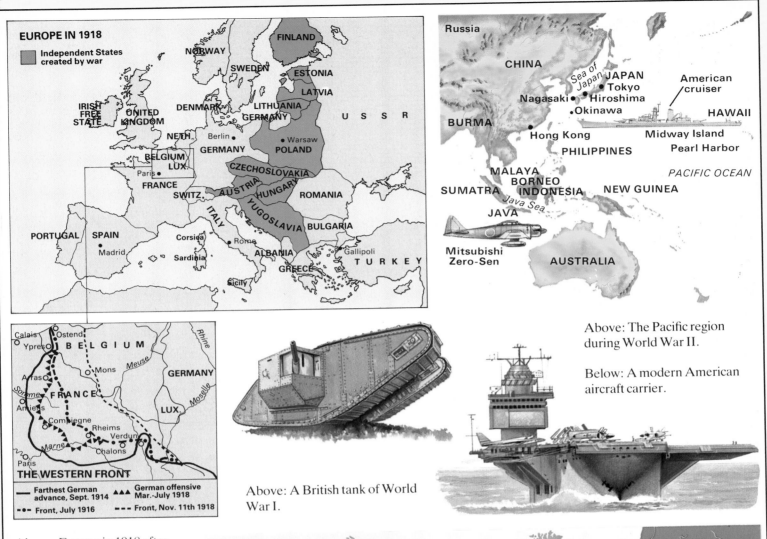

**EUROPE IN 1918**

Independent States created by war

NORWAY
FINLAND
SWEDEN
ESTONIA
LATVIA
LITHUANIA
IRISH FREE STATE
UNITED KINGDOM
DENMARK
GERMANY
U S S R
NETH.
Berlin
Warsaw
POLAND
GERMANY
BELGIUM
LUX.
Paris
FRANCE
CZECHOSLOVAKIA
AUSTRIA
HUNGARY
SWITZ.
ROMANIA
YUGOSLAVIA
ITALY
BULGARIA
PORTUGAL
SPAIN
Corsica
Madrid
Rome
Sardinia
ALBANIA
Gallipoli
GREECE
Sicily
T U R K E Y

Russia
CHINA
Sea of Japan
JAPAN
Tokyo
Nagasaki
Hiroshima
Okinawa
American cruiser
HAWAII
BURMA
Hong Kong
Midway Island
Pearl Harbor
PHILIPPINES
MALAYA
BORNEO
PACIFIC OCEAN
SUMATRA
INDONESIA
NEW GUINEA
Java Sea
JAVA
Mitsubishi Zero-Sen
AUSTRALIA

Calais
Ostend
Ypres
B E L G I U M
Rhine
Mons
Meuse
Arras
GERMANY
Somme
F R A N C E
LUX.
Amiens
Compiegne
Rheims
Moselle
Verdun
Marne
Chalons
Paris
**THE WESTERN FRONT**

— Farthest German advance, Sept. 1914
▲▲▲ German offensive Mar.-July 1918
•—• Front, July 1916
- - - Front, Nov. 11th 1918

Above: The Pacific region during World War II.

Below: A modern American aircraft carrier.

Above: A British tank of World War I.

Above: Europe in 1918 after World War I. Most of the battles took place along a great line of trenches and barbed wire known as the "Western Front." It stretched from the Belgian coast to the Alps, with Germany and its allies on one side, and France, Britain, and their allies on the other. Thousands of men died just gaining a few yards of ground for their side.

Right: The map shows the countries of NATO, the North Atlantic Treaty Organization (which also includes the United States of America and Canada) and of the Communist Warsaw Pact countries. Since World War II these two groups have opposed each other in what is called the "Cold War."

Iceland

← United States, Canada
NATO countries
Warsaw Pact countries

Norway
Sweden
Finland
USSR
United Kingdom
Denmark
W. Germany
E. Germany
Poland
Netherlands
Belgium
Luxembourg
Czechoslovakia
France
Austria
Hungary
Romania
Switzerland
Yugoslavia
Portugal
Spain
Italy
Albania
Bulgaria
Turkey
Greece

# The Middle East

The Middle East lies where the continents of Europe, Africa, and Asia meet, and much of the trade between East and West has had to pass through its frontiers. As a result, what happens there has always been very important to the great trading nations of the world. Much of the area is desert. Little rain falls there, and what farming there is depends on irrigation.

For hundreds of years most of the Middle East was part of the great Ottoman Empire. The people were almost all Muslims and they spoke Arabic. Then the Ottoman Empire lost its power. Egypt came under British and French control; it became especially important when the Suez Canal was built to link the Mediterranean Sea with the Red Sea, and through it the Indian Ocean. This made it far quicker for ships of all nations to sail to India and the East.

The Middle East was the birthplace of three of the world's greatest religions—Judaism, Christianity and Islam. The area known until recently as Palestine, running along the east coast of the Mediterranean, was the home of the Jews until most of them were driven out by the Romans.

In 1917 it was suggested that a Jewish "homeland" should be set up in the area, where Jews from all over the world could come and settle. This did not please the Muslims who had lived there for hundreds of years. Fighting followed and the state of Israel was set up. Many Palestinians fled to the neighboring Arab countries where they still live as refugees. But they want to go back to their old home. They are given support by other Muslims and there have been three wars and a great deal of other fighting in recent years.

Right: Many Muslims in the Middle East think people are taking up Western ways too fast, and are forgetting the teachings of the *Koran*. In 1979 a religious leader called the Ayatollah Khomeini led a revolution in Iran and set up a new religious state. Here a crowd of Iranians wave banners showing portraits of the Ayatollah.

Below: Oil has brought great wealth in the Middle East but many people still live in their traditional way. Here a shepherd guides his flock while oil wells flare in the background.

Left: This statue shows the Turkish leader Mustapha Kemal. He is also called Atatürk, which means "father of the Turks." He became president of Turkey after World War I, when the Ottoman Empire finally broke up. Life in Turkey had hardly changed for hundreds of years under the Ottomans, and Kemal did all he could to bring his country up to date.

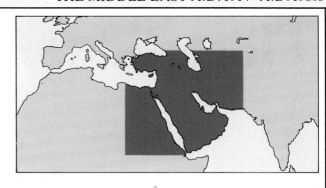

Right: The mosque called the Dome of the Rock in Jerusalem. This is a holy city for Jews, Christians, and Muslims, who have fought over it often in the past. Now it is part of the Jewish state of Israel. The Muslim Arabs bitterly resent this.

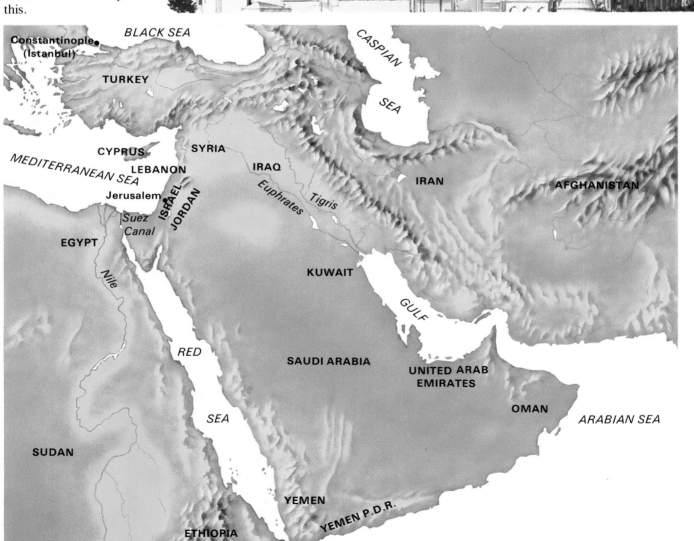

Constantinople (Istanbul)

BLACK SEA

CASPIAN SEA

TURKEY

CYPRUS

MEDITERRANEAN SEA

SYRIA

LEBANON

IRAQ

IRAN

AFGHANISTAN

Jerusalem

ISRAEL

JORDAN

Euphrates

Tigris

Suez Canal

EGYPT

Nile

KUWAIT

GULF

RED

SAUDI ARABIA

UNITED ARAB EMIRATES

OMAN

ARABIAN SEA

SEA

SUDAN

YEMEN

YEMEN P.D.R.

ETHIOPIA

# The World Today

In the 1700s and 1800s, several European countries built up large empires scattered over many parts of the world. Today these empires have largely disappeared. Since World War II, most of the colonies have gained independence.

Some countries have had a difficult time since independence. In India there was great trouble between the Hindus and the Muslims. Neither was willing to be ruled by the other. The country became split into Hindu India and Muslim Pakistan in the northeast and northwest. Many Hindus and Muslims left their homes to move to regions ruled by people of their own faith and there were terrible massacres in which hundreds of thousands of people were killed.

Most of the countries of the British Empire have stayed linked together as members of the Commonwealth of Nations. They still all share the leadership of the British monarch.

The former colonies were mostly in Africa, Asia, and the West Indies. People in these countries are much poorer than those in most other parts of the world. These poorer nations are often called the developing countries; the others are developed countries.

People in developing countries have many problems. Food is often in short supply and there are few schools, doctors, and hospitals. They can expect to live perhaps only half as long as the people in developed nations. These countries do not have many industries and most of their people are farmers, who grow just enough to feed their families. If droughts, floods, or pests destroy the crops, there are famines and thousands of people die of starvation. Despite this, the populations of developing countries are growing much faster than those of developed countries.

In many parts of the world people are still very poor. They can barely get enough to eat and live in very simple houses. They have to walk a long way to the nearest source of water, which has to be carried back to their village (below left).

In rich countries people can easily buy things from all different parts of the world. The supermarket dairy counter (below) is typical of large stores. It contains food from many different countries.

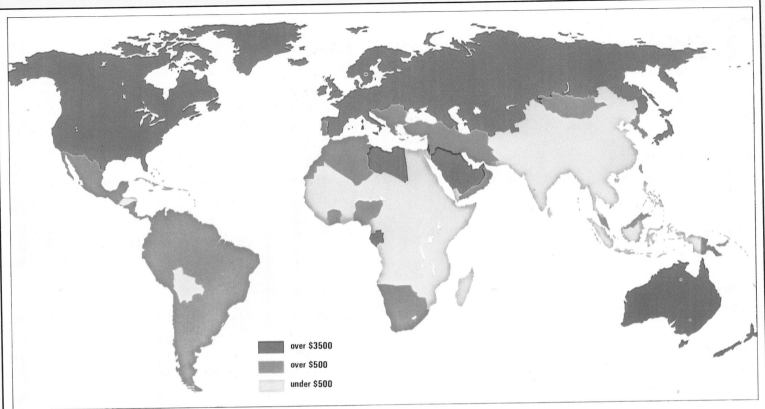

over $3500

over $500

under $500

Above: This map shows the average income of people living in the world today. In some ways it is misleading, since the figures are worked out country by country; and in some nations a few people are very rich while most people are quite poor. But it does show the general difference between the wealthy industrial countries and the poorer developing countries of Africa and Asia.

Below: This is an "equal area" map in which mapmakers have flattened the curve of the Earth's surface, so that you can compare the area of one country with that of another. It shows the states of the world today. In the past 50 years the number of independent countries has more than doubled. Most remaining colonies (dependencies) are small, such as Hong Kong and the Falklands.

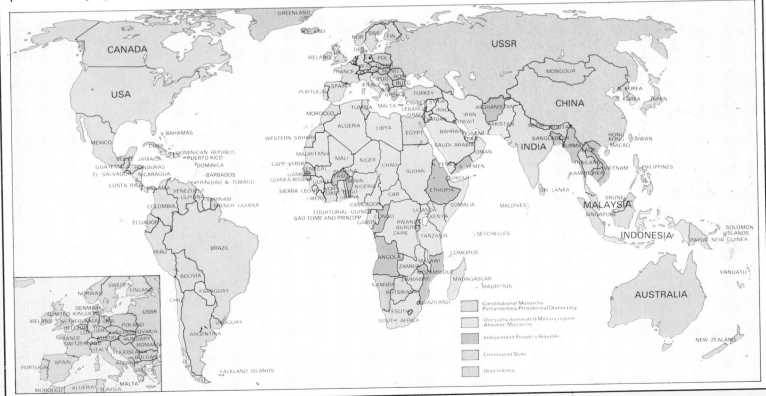

Constitutional Monarchy
Parliamentary-Presidential Democracy

One party dominated Military regime
Absolute Monarchy

Independent People's Republic

Communist State

Dependency

# Time Chart

200 B.C. *means 200 years* before *the birth of Christ.*
A.D. 200 *means 200 years* after *the birth of Christ.*
c.1450 *means* circa 1450, *or* approximately 1450.

| EUROPE | | AMERICAS | | ASIA | |
|---|---|---|---|---|---|
| **B.C.** | | **B.C.** | | **B.C.** | |
| *c.* 20,000 | Cave paintings in France and Spain | | | | |
| *c.* 6500 | First farming in Greece | | | *c.* 8000 | Agriculture develops in the Middle East |
| | | | | *c.* 6000 | Rice cultivated in Thailand |
| | | | | *c.* 4000 | Bronze casting begins in Near East |
| *c.* 2600 | Beginnings of Minoan civilization in Crete | *c.* 3000 | First pottery in Mexico | *c.* 3000 | Developent of major cities in Sumer |
| *c.* 1600 | Beginnings of Mycenaean civilization in Greece | *c.* 2000 | First metal working in Peru | *c.* 2750 | Growth of civilizations in Indus Valley |
| *c.* 1450 | Destruction of Minoan Crete | | | *c.* 2200 | Hsia dynasty in China |
| *c.* 1200 | Collapse of Mycenaean Empire | | | *c.* 1750 | Collapse of Indus Valley civilization |
| *c.* 1100 | Phoenician supremacy in Mediterranean Sea | | | *c.* 1500 | Rise of Shang dynasty in China |
| 900–750 | Rise of city-states in Greece | | | *c.* 1200 | Beginning of Jewish religion |
| 776 | First Olympic Games | | | *c.* 1050 | Shang dynasty overthrown by Chou in China |
| 753 | Foundation of Rome (traditional date) | | | *c.* 770 | Chou dynasty weakening |
| | | | | *c.* 720 | Height of Assyrian power |
| | | | | *c.* 650 | First iron used in China |
| 510 | Foundation of Roman Republic | | | 586 | Babylonian captivity of Jews |
| 477–405 | Athenian supremacy in Aegean | | | | |
| 431–404 | War between Athens and Sparta (Peloponnesian War) | | | 483–221 | "Warring States" period in China |
| 290 | Roman conquest of central Italy | | | *c.* 320 | Mauryan Empire in India |
| 264–146 | Punic Wars between Rome and Carthage | | | 221 | Ch'in dynasty |
| | | | | 202 | Han dynasty re-unites China |
| 146 | Greece comes under Roman rule | | | | |
| **A.D.** | | **A.D.** | | **A.D.** | |
| | | | | *c.* 0 | Buddhism introduced to China from India |
| 43 | Roman invasion of Britain | | | 25 | Han dynasty restored in China |
| 116 | Emperor Trajan extends Roman Empire to Euphrates | | | 45 | Beginning of St. Paul's missionary journeys |
| 238 | Beginnings of raids by Goths | | | 132 | Jewish rebellion against Rome |
| 293 | Division of Roman Empire by Diocletian | | | 220 | End of Han dynasty; China splits into three states |
| 370 | Huns from Asia invade Europe | | | | |
| 410 | Visigoths sack Rome | | | | |
| 449 | Angles, Saxons, and Jutes invade Britain | *c.* 300 | Rise of Mayan civilization in Central America | 330 | Capital of Roman Empire transferred to Constantinople |
| 486 | Frankish kingdom founded by Clovis | *c.* 400 | Incas established on parts of South American Pacific coast | 350 | Huns invade Persia and India |
| 497 | Franks converted to Christianity | | | 407–553 | First Mongol Empire |

| AFRICA | PEOPLE | INVENTIONS & DISCOVERIES |
|---|---|---|
| **B.C.** | **B.C.** | **B.C.** |
| | | *c.* **6000** First known pottery and textiles |
| *c.* **5000** Agricultural settlements in Egypt | | *c.* **5000** First known use of irrigation |
| | | *c.* **4000** Invention of plow and sail |
| *c.* **3100** King Menes unites Egypt | | *c.* **3100** First known use of writing on clay tablets |
| *c.* **2685** Beginning of "Old Kingdom" in Egypt | | *c.* **2590** Cheops builds Great Pyramid at Giza in Egypt |
| *c.* **1570** Beginning of "New Kingdom" in Egypt | *c.* **2650** Death of King Zoser of Egypt, for whom first pyramid was built | |
| | **1792–50** Rule of Hammurabi in Babylon | |
| | **1361–52** Rule of Tutankhamun in Egypt | |
| | **1304–1237** Rule of Ramses II in Egypt | *c.* **1100** Phoenicians develop alphabet |
| **814** Carthage founded by Phoenicians | **1198–66** Reign of Ramses III, last great Pharaoh | |
| | *c.* **605–520** Lao-tzu, founder of Taoism | |
| | **563–479** Siddhartha Gautama (the Buddha) | |
| | **551–479** Confucius, Chinese thinker | |
| | **427–347** Plato, Greek thinker | |
| | **384–322** Aristotle, Greek thinker | *c.* **214** Building of Great Wall of China |
| | **356–323** Alexander the Great | |
| | **100–44** Julius Caesar | |
| **A.D.** | **A.D.** | **A.D.** |
| | **63 B.C.– 14 A.D.** Augustus (Octavian), first Roman Emperor | |
| **30** Egypt becomes Roman province | *c.* **4 B.C.– c. A.D. 30** Jesus Christ, founder of Christianity | |
| | **54–68** Reign of Emperor Nero | **142** First stone bridge built over river Tiber |
| | **97–117** Reign of Emperor Trajan | *c.* **105** First use of paper in China |
| | | *c.* **271** Magnetic compass in use in China |
| | **306–337** Reign of Emperor Constantine | *c.* **300** Foot stirrup for riding invented |
| | **340–420** St. Jerome, Bible translator | |
| | **379–395** Theodosius I, Roman Emperor in the East | |
| **429–535** Vandal kingdom in northern Africa | **480–543** St. Benedict, founder of first monastery | |

| EUROPE | AMERICAS | ASIA & OCEANIA |
|---|---|---|
| | | **552** Buddhism introduced to Japan |
| **597** St. Augustine's mission to England | **c. 600** Height of Mayan civilization | **618** China re-united under T'ang dynasty |
| | | **635** Muslims begin conquest of Syria and Persia |
| | | **674** Muslim conquest reaches river Indus |
| **711** Muslim conquest of Spain | | |
| **793** Viking raids begin | | |
| **800** Charlemagne crowned Emperor in Rome | | **821** Conquest of Tibet by Chinese |
| **843** Partition of Carolingian Empire at Treaty of Verdun | | |
| **874** First Viking settlers in Iceland | | |
| **886** King Alfred defeats Danish King Guthrum. Danelaw established in England | | **907** Last T'ang Emperor deposed in China |
| **911** Vikings granted duchy of Normandy by Frankish king | **c. 990** Expansion of Inca Empire | **939** Civil wars in Japan |
| | | **960** Sung dynasty re-unites China |
| **1016** King Cnut rules England, Denmark and Norway | | **1054** Break between Greek and Latin Christian churches begins |
| **1066** William of Normandy defeats Anglo-Saxons at Hastings | | |
| **1071** Normans conquer Byzantine Italy | | **1071** Seljuk Turks conquer most of Asia Minor |
| **1096–99** First Crusade | **1100s** Inca family under Manco Capac settle in Cuzco | **c. 1100** Polynesian Islands colonized |
| **1147–49** Second Crusade | **1151** End of Toltec Empire in Mexico | |
| **1170** Murder of Thómas à Becket at Canterbury | **1168** Aztecs leave Chimoztoc Valley | **1156–89** Civil wars in Japan |
| **1189–93** Third Crusade | | **1174** Saladin conquers Syria |
| **1198** Innocent III elected Pope | | **1187** Saladin captures Jerusalem |
| | | **1190** Temujin begins to create Empire in eastern Asia |
| **1202–04** Fourth Crusade leads to capture of Constantinople | | |
| **1215** King John of England signs Magna Carta | | **1206** Temujin proclaimed Genghis Khan |
| **1217–22** Fifth Crusade | | **1210** Mongols invade China |
| **1228–29** Sixth Crusade | | **1234** Mongols destroy Chinese Empire |
| **1236** Mongols invade Russia | | **1261** Greek Empire restored at Constantinople |
| **1241** Mongols invade Poland, Hungary, Bohemia, then withdraw | | **1279** Mongols conquer southern China |
| **1248–54** Seventh Crusade | | **1281** Mongols fail in attempt to conquer Japan |
| **1250** Collapse of imperial power in Germany and Italy on death of Frederick II | | **1299** Ottoman Turks begin expansion |
| **1270–72** Eighth Crusade | | |

| AFRICA | | PEOPLE | | INVENTIONS & DISCOVERIES | |
|---|---|---|---|---|---|
| 533–552 | Justinian restores Roman power in North Africa | 527–565 | Reign of Emperor Justinian | c. 520 | Rise of mathematics in India. Invention of decimal system. |
| | | 570–632 | Muhammad, founder of Islam | | |
| | | 590–604 | Reign of Pope Gregory I | | |
| 641 | Conquest of Egypt by Muslims | | | | |
| | | 673–735 | Venerable Bede, English monk and historian | | |
| c. 700 | Rise of Empire of Ghana | 742–814 | Charlemagne | | |
| | | | | c. 730 | First printing in China |
| | | | | c. 750 | Paper-making spreads to Muslim world |
| | | | | 760 | Muslims adopt numerals |
| | | | | 788 | Great Mosque built at Cordoba in Spain |
| 850 | Acropolis of Zimbabwe built | | | 850 | First printed book in China |
| | | | | 860 | Discovery of Iceland by Vikings |
| | | | | 982 | Erik the Red discovers Greenland |
| 920–1050 | Height of Ghana Empire | 987–996 | Reign of Hugh Capet, first King of France | c. 1000 | Vikings discover America |
| 969 | Fatamids conquer Egypt and found Cairo | 980–1037 | Avicenna, great Arab physician | c. 1000 | Great age of Chinese painting |
| c. 1000 | First Iron Age settlement at Zimbabwe | 1066–87 | Reign of William I, King of England | c. 1045 | Movable type printing invented in China |
| | | 1138–93 | Saladin, Sultan of Egypt and Syria | c. 1100 | Foundation of first universities in Europe |
| | | 1155–90 | Reign of Emperor Frederick I | | |
| c. 1150 | Beginnings of Yoruba city-states (Nigeria) | 1154–89 | Reign of Henry II of England | | |
| | | 1162–1227 | Genghis Khan | 1161 | Explosives used in China |
| 1174 | Saladin conquers Egypt | 1170–1221 | St. Dominic, founder of Dominicans | 1167 | Foundation of Oxford University |
| | | 1182–1226 | St. Francis of Assisi, founder of Franciscans | | |
| c. 1200 | Rise of Empire of Mali in West Africa | | | | |
| c. 1200 | Emergence of Hausa city-states (Nigeria) | | | 1209 | Foundation of Cambridge University |
| 1240 | Collapse of Empire of Ghana | 1214–94 | Roger Bacon, English philosopher | | |
| | | 1216–94 | Kublai Khan | | |
| | | 1225–74 | Thomas Aquinas, Italian philosopher | | |
| | | 1265–1321 | Dante, Italian poet | 1271–95 | Journey to China by Marco Polo, father and uncle |
| c. 1300 | Emergence of Ife Kingdom (West Africa) | 1254–1324 | Marco Polo, traveler | 1290 | Spectacles invented in Italy |
| | | 1267–1337 | Giotto, Italian painter | | |

| EUROPE | | AMERICAS | | ASIA & OCEANIA | |
|---|---|---|---|---|---|
| 1305 | Papacy moves from Rome to Avignon | | | | |
| | | c. 1300 | Inca Roca takes title of Sapa Inca | | |
| 1337–1453 | Hundred Years' War between France and England | 1325 | Rise of Aztecs. Founding of Tenochtitlán | 1336 | Revolution in Japan |
| 1346 | English defeat French at Battle of Crecy | | | c. 1341 | Black Death begins |
| 1348 | Black Death reaches Europe | | | | |
| 1356 | English defeat French at Battle of Poitiers | | | | |
| | | 1370 | Expansion of Chimu kingdom | 1363 | Tamerlane begins conquest of Asia |
| | | c. 1375 | Beginning of Aztec expansion | 1368 | Ming dynasty founded in China |
| 1378–1417 | Great Schism: (break between Rome and Avignon) rival popes elected | | | | |
| 1381 | Peasants' Revolt in England | 1438 | Inca Empire established in Peru | | |
| 1385 | Independence of Portugal | 1440–69 | Montezuma rules Aztecs | 1398 | Tamerlane ravages kingdom of Delhi |
| | | 1450 | Incas conquer Chimu kingdom | 1401 | Tamerlane conquers Damascus and Baghdad |
| 1415 | Henry V defeats French at Battle of Agincourt | | | 1402 | Tamerlane overruns Ottoman Empire |
| | | | | 1421 | Peking becomes capital of China |
| 1453 | England loses all French possessions except Calais | | | 1453 | Ottoman Turks capture Constantinople |
| 1455–85 | Wars of the Roses in England | | | | |
| 1492 | Last Muslims in Spain conquered by Christians | | | | |
| 1517 | Martin Luther nails 95 "theses" to church door at Wittenberg | 1486–1502 | Aztec Empire reaches sea | 1516 | Ottomans overrun Syria, Egypt, and Arabia |
| | | 1493 | Spanish make first settlement in New World (Hispaniola) | | |
| 1519 | Zwingli leads Reformation in Switzerland | 1502–20 | Aztec conquests under Montezuma II | | |
| 1529 | Reformation Parliament begins in England | c. 1510 | First African slaves taken to America | | |
| 1532 | Calvin starts Protestant movement in France | 1521 | Cortes conquers Aztec capital, Tenochtitlán | 1526 | Foundation of Mughal Empire |
| 1536 | Suppression of monasteries begins in England | 1533 | Pizarro conquers Peru | 1533 | Ivan the Terrible succeeds to Russian throne |
| 1545 | Council of Trent marks start of Counter-Reformation | 1535 | Spaniards explore Chile | | |
| 1558 | England loses Calais to French | | | 1556 | Ivan the Terrible conquers Volga basin |
| 1562–98 | Wars of Religion in France | | | 1565 | Mughal power extended |
| 1571 | Battle of Lepanto: end of Turkish sea power | | | | |
| 1572 | Dutch revolt against Spain | | | | |
| 1588 | Spanish Armada defeated by English | | | | |

| AFRICA | PEOPLE | INVENTIONS & DISCOVERIES |
|---|---|---|
| | | **1315** Silk industry developed in Lyons, France |
| **1352** Arab geographer Ibn Battuta explores Sahara Desert | **1320–84** John Wycliffe, English religious reformer<br>**1336–1405** Tamerlane, Mongol Emperor<br>**1340–1400** Geoffrey Chaucer, English poet | |
| | **1369–1415** John Huss, German religious reformer | |
| | **1377–1446** Brunelleschi, Italian architect<br>**1386–1466** Donatello, Italian sculptor<br>**1394–1460** Henry the Navigator<br>**1412–31** Joan of Arc of France | **1405** Chinese voyages in the Indian Ocean |
| **1415** Beginning of Portugal's African Empire | **1422–91** William Caxton, English printer<br>**1443–96** Francis Drake, English sailor<br>**1451–1506** Christopher Columbus<br>**1452–1519** Leonardo da Vinci, Renaissance artist<br>**1469–1524** Vasco da Gama, Portuguese explorer<br>**1466–1536** Erasmus, Renaissance writer<br>**1475–1564** Michelangelo, Renaissance artist | **1454** Gutenburg prints first book from movable type (in Europe)<br>**1488** Bartolomeu Dias sails around Cape of Good Hope<br>**1492** Columbus reaches West Indies<br>**1497** John Cabot reaches Newfoundland<br>**1498** Vasco da Gama reaches India around Cape of Good Hope |
| **1450** Height of Songhai Empire in West Africa<br>**1482** Portuguese settle Gold Coast (now Ghana)<br>**1492** Spain begins conquest of North African coast<br>**1505** Portuguese establish trading posts in East Africa | **1480–1521** Ferdinand Magellan, Portuguese explorer<br>**1483–1520** Raphael, Renaissance painter<br>**1483–1546** Martin Luther, German religious reformer<br>**1491–1556** Ignatius Loyola, Spanish founder of Jesuits<br>**1497–1543** Hans Holbein, German painter<br>**1500–33** Atahualpa, last Inca ruler<br>**1505–72** John Knox, Scottish Protestant reformer<br>**1509–64** John Calvin, French religious reformer<br>**1512–94** Mercator, Flemish cartographer | **1501** Vespucci explores Brazilian coast<br>**1522** One of Magellan's ships completes first circumnavigation of world<br>**1525** Potato introduced to Europe<br>**1535** Cartier navigates St. Lawrence River<br>**1543** Copernicus declares that Earth revolves around Sun |
| **1546** Destruction of Mali Empire by Songhai<br>**1570** Bornu Empire in the Sudan flourishes<br>**1571** Portuguese establish colony in Angola (Southern Africa)<br>**1591** Moroccans destroy Songhai Empire | **1547–1616** Cervantes, Spanish writer<br>**1548–1614** El Greco, Spanish painter<br>**1564–1616** William Shakespeare, English playwright<br>**1564–1642** Galileo, Italian astronomer<br>**1577–1640** Rubens, Flemish painter<br>**1588–1679** Thomas Hobbes, English thinker<br>**1596–1650** Descartes, French thinker | **1559** Tobacco introduced to Europe<br><br>**1577–80** Drakes sails around world<br>**1582** Introduction of Gregorian calendar |

| EUROPE | | AMERICAS | | ASIA & OCEANIA | |
|---|---|---|---|---|---|
| 1600 | English East India Company founded | | | | |
| 1605 | Gunpowder Plot | 1607 | First English settlement in America | | |
| 1609 | Dutch win freedom from Spain | 1608 | French colonists found Quebec | | |
| 1618–48 | Thirty Years' War | | | | |
| | | 1620 | Puritans (Pilgrim Fathers) land in New England | | |
| 1642–46 | English Civil War | 1624 | Dutch settle New Amsterdam | 1630s | Japan isolates itself from rest of world |
| 1649 | Execution of Charles I in London | | | | |
| | | 1644 | New Amsterdam seized by British and re-named New York | 1644 | Ch'ing dynasty founded in China by Manchus |
| | | 1654 | Portuguese take Brazil from Dutch | | |
| 1688 | England's "Glorious Revolution" | | | 1690 | Foundation of Calcutta by British |
| | | 1693 | Gold discovered in Brazil | | |
| 1701 | Act of Settlement in Britain | | | 1707 | Break up of Mughal Empire |
| 1701–14 | War of Spanish Succession | | | 1724 | Hyderabad in India gains freedom from Mughals |
| 1704 | Battle of Blenheim | | | | |
| 1707 | Union of England and Scotland | | | | |
| 1713 | Treaty of Utrecht | | | | |
| 1740–48 | War of Austrian Succession | | | | |
| 1746 | Jacobites defeated at Culloden in Scotland | | | 1757 | Battle of Plassey establishes British rule in India |
| 1756–63 | Seven Years' War | | | | |
| | | 1759 | British capture Quebec from French | | |
| | | 1765 | Stamp Act in American colonies | | |
| | | 1773 | Boston Tea Party | | |
| | | 1775–83 | American War of Independence | 1775 | Peasant uprising in Russia |
| | | 1776 | Declaration of American Independence | 1783 | India Act gives Britain control of India |
| 1789 | French Revolution | 1789 | Washington becomes first U.S. President | | |
| 1804 | Napoleon proclaimed Emperor | 1791 | Slave revolt in Haiti | 1788 | British colony founded at Botany Bay, Australia |
| 1805 | Battle of Trafalgar | 1803 | Louisiana Purchase doubles size of U.S.A. | 1799 | Napoleon invades Syria |
| 1812 | Napoleon's Russian campaign | 1808–28 | Independence movements in South America | 1804–15 | Serbs revolt against Turkey |
| | | | | 1819 | British found Singapore |
| 1815 | Napoleon defeated at Waterloo Congress of Vienna | 1819 | Spain cedes Florida to U.S. | 1830–54 | Russia conquers Kazakhstan |
| | | | | 1840 | Britain annexes New Zealand |
| 1821–29 | Greek War of Independence | 1836 | Texas independent of Mexico | 1842 | Hong Kong ceded to Britain |
| 1830 | Revolutions in France, Germany, Poland, and Italy | 1840 | Union of Upper and Lower Canada | 1845–48 | Anglo-Sikh wars in India |
| | | | | 1850/56 | Australia and New Zealand granted responsible governments |
| 1846 | Irish potato famine | 1846–48 | War between U.S.A. and Mexico | | |
| 1846 | Britain repeals Corn Laws | | | | |
| 1848 | Year of Revolutions | 1848 | California Gold Rush begins | 1854 | Trade treaty between Japan and U.S. |
| 1851 | Great Exhibition in London | | | | |
| 1854–56 | Crimean War | | | 1857 | Indian Mutiny |

| AFRICA | PEOPLE | INVENTIONS & DISCOVERIES |
|---|---|---|
| | 1602–61 Mazarin, French statesman | |
| | 1606–69 Rembrandt, Dutch painter | |
| | 1608–74 John Milton, English poet | 1608 Invention of telescope |
| | 1622–73 Molière, French dramatist | 1618 Imbert (French) reaches Timbuktu |
| | 1642–1727 Isaac Newton, English scientist | |
| | 1643–1715 Reign of Louis XIV | |
| | 1650–1722 Duke of Marlborough | |
| | 1682–1725 Reign of Peter the Great | |
| | 1685–1750 J. S. Bach, German composer | 1642 Tasman discovers New Zealand and Tasmania |
| | 1694–1778 Voltaire, French writer | 1643 Invention of barometer |
| | 1703–91 John Wesley, English preacher | |
| 1652 Foundations of Cape Colony by Dutch | 1706–90 Benjamin Franklin, American inventor | |
| | 1712–78 J. J. Rousseau, French philosopher | 1698 Thomas Savery invents steam pump |
| 1686 French annex Madagascar | 1725–74 Robert Clive, ruler in India | |
| | 1728–79 James Cook, British explorer | |
| | 1732–99 George Washington, American statesman | 1709 Darby pioneers iron smelting |
| 1705 Turks overthrown in Tunis | 1743–1826 Thomas Jefferson, American statesman | 1712 Thomas Newcomen's steam engine |
| | 1756–91 Mozart, Austrian composer | 1728 Bering discovers Bering Strait |
| | 1769–1821 Napoleon Bonaparte | 1733 John Kay's flying shuttle |
| | 1769–1850 Duke of Wellington | 1752 Franklin's lightning conductor |
| | 1770–1827 Beethoven, German composer | 1764 Hargreave's spinning jenny |
| | 1770–1850 Wordsworth, English poet | 1765 James Watt's steam engine |
| | 1776–1837 John Constable, English painter | 1768 Cook begins Pacific exploration |
| | 1783–1830 Simón Bolívar, "Liberator" | 1781 Planet Uranus discovered |
| | 1788–1850 Robert Peel, English statesman | 1782 Watt's double acting steam engine |
| | 1806–59 Brunel, British engineer | 1785 Cartwright's power loom |
| | 1809–65 Abraham Lincoln, American statesman | 1793 Eli Whitney's cotton gin |
| 1787 British acquire Sierra Leone | 1809–82 Charles Darwin, English naturalist | 1804 Trevithick develops the steam locomotive |
| 1798 Napoleon attacks Egypt | 1810–61 Cavour, Italian unifier | 1805 Mungo Park explores Niger River |
| 1802–11 Portuguese cross Africa | 1812–70 Charles Dickens, English novelist | |
| 1807 British abolish slave trade | 1815–98 Bismarck, German statesman | |
| 1811 Muhammad Ali takes control in Egypt | 1818–83 Karl Marx, German philosopher | |
| 1818 Zulu Empire founded in southern Africa | 1822–95 Louis Pasteur, French scientist | 1815 Davy's miners' safety lamp |
| 1822 Liberia founded for free slaves | 1828–1910 Leo Tolstoy, Russian writer | 1825 First passenger steam railway |
| 1830 French begin conquest of Algeria | 1837–1901 Reign of Queen Victoria | 1825 Neilson's blast furnace |
| | 1840–1926 Claude Monet, French painter | 1831 Faraday's dynamo |
| 1835–37 Great Trek of Boers in South Africa | 1840–1917 Rodin, French sculptor | 1844 Invention of safety match |
| | 1856–1939 Sigmund Freud, Austrian psychoanalyst | 1846 Planet Neptune discovered |
| | 1858–1928 Emmeline Pankhurst, women's rights leader | 1853–6 Livingstone crosses Africa |
| | 1860–1904 Anton Chekhov, Russian playwright | 1855 Bessemer's converter |
| 1860 French expansion in West Africa | | 1859 Lake Tanganyika discovered |

| EUROPE | | AMERICAS | | ASIA & OCEANIA | |
|---|---|---|---|---|---|
| 1861 | Kingdom of Italy set up | 1861–65 | American Civil War | 1877 | Victoria becomes Empress of India |
| 1867 | North German confederation | 1865 | Abraham Lincoln assassinated | 1885 | Indian National Congress formed |
| 1870–71 | Franco–Prussian War | 1867 | Dominion of Canada formed | 1886 | British annex Burma |
| 1871 | Proclamation of German Empire | 1876 | Battle of Little Big Horn | 1894–5 | Sino–Japanese War |
| | | 1898 | Spanish–American War | 1901 | Unification of Australia |
| 1872–1914 | Triple Alliance between Germany, Austria and Italy | 1903 | Panama Canal Zone to U.S.A. | 1906 | Revolution in Persia |
| 1904 | Anglo–French Entente | 1911 | Revolution in Mexico | 1910 | Japan annexes Korea |
| 1905 | First revolution in Russia | 1914 | Panama Canal opens | 1911–49 | Chinese Revolution |
| 1912–13 | Balkan Wars | 1917 | U.S. enters World War I | 1917 | Balfour Declaration promises Jewish homeland |
| 1914–18 | World War I | | | | |
| 1917 | Russian Revolution | | | 1922 | Republic proclaimed in Turkey |
| 1919 | Treaty of Versailles | 1920 | U.S. refuses to join League of Nations | 1926 | Chiang Kai-shek unites China |
| 1920 | League of Nations established | 1929 | Wall Street crash | 1931 | Japanese occupy Manchuria |
| 1922 | Irish Free State created Mussolini takes power in Italy | 1933 | Roosevelt introduces New Deal in U.S.A. | 1934 | Mao Zedong's (Mao Tse-tung) Long March |
| 1926 | General Strike in Britain | 1941 | U.S. enters World War II | 1937 | Japanese capture Peking |
| 1933 | Hitler becomes German Chancellor | | | 1940 | Japan allies with Germany |
| | | | | 1945 | First A-bombs dropped on Japan |
| 1936–39 | Spanish Civil War | | | 1946–49 | Civil war in China |
| 1939–45 | World War II | | | 1948/9 | First Arab–Israeli War |
| 1945 | United Nations established | | | 1947 | India and Pakistan independent |
| 1949 | Formation of NATO | | | | |
| 1955 | Warsaw Pact signed | | | 1950–53 | Korean War |
| 1958 | European Economic Community (EEC) set up | 1959 | Cuban Revolution | 1954–75 | Vietnam War |
| | | 1962 | Cuba missile crisis | 1956 | Second Arab–Israeli War |
| 1961 | Berlin Wall built | 1963 | President Kennedy assassinated | 1957 | Malaysia independent |
| 1963 | Nuclear Test Ban Treaty | | | 1962 | Sino–Indian War |
| 1968 | U.S.S.R. invades Czechoslovakia | 1964–73 | U.S. involvement in Vietnam War | 1967 | Third Arab–Israeli War |
| 1973 | Britain, Eire, and Denmark join EEC | 1970–73 | Chilean Revolution | 1971 | East Pakistan becomes Bangladesh |
| 1975 | Monarchy restored in Spain | 1974 | Resignation of President Nixon | 1973 | Fourth Arab–Israeli War |
| 1978 | John Paul II elected as first non-Italian Pope for 450 years | 1978 | U.S. agrees to diplomatic relations with China and ends those with Taiwan | 1974 | Portuguese African colonies independent |
| 1979 | Margaret Thatcher first woman prime minister of Britain | 1981 | U.S. hostages in Iran freed | 1975 | Outbreak of civil war in Lebanon |
| 1980 | President Tito of Yugoslavia dies. Polish Solidarity trade union, led by Lech Walesa, confronts Communist government | 1982 | Argentines invade Falkland Islands | 1978 | Fifth Arab–Israeli War |
| | | 1983 | U.S. troops invade Grenada | 1979 | Soviet invasion of Afghanistan |
| | | 1986 | U.S. raid on Libya Nuclear arms talks resume between U.S.A. and U.S.S.R. | 1979 | Shah of Iran deposed. An Islamic republic is declared |
| 1981 | Greece becomes 10th member of the EEC | | | 1980 | Iran–Iraq war (Gulf War) |
| 1985 | Mikhail Gorbachev elected new Soviet leader | | | 1982 | Israel invades Lebanon to drive Palestine Liberation Organization from the country |
| 1986 | Chernobyl nuclear reactor explosion, U.S.S.R. Prime Minister Palme of Sweden assassinated | | | 1984 | Indira Gandhi, Indian prime minister, assassinated |
| | | | | 1985 | World's worst industrial disaster in Bhopal, India |
| | | | | 1986 | Overthrow of Marcos régime in Philippines |
| | | | | 1987 | Civil war in Lebanon continues. Gulf War intensifies |

| AFRICA | PEOPLE | INVENTIONS & DISCOVERIES |
|---|---|---|
| 1869 Opening of Suez Canal | 1863–1947 Henry Ford, U.S. car maker | 1862 Gatling's rapid fire gun |
| 1875 Disraeli buys Suez Canal shares | 1866–1925 Sun Yat-sen, Chinese leader | 1866 Nobel invents dynamite |
| 1879 Zulu War | 1868–1912 Robert Scott, English explorer | 1869 First trans-continental railroad completed in U.S.A. |
| 1882 British occupy Egypt | 1870–1924 Lenin, Russian revolutionary | |
| 1884 Germany acquires African colonies | 1871–1937 Ernest Rutherford, New Zealand physicist | 1871 Stanley finds Livingstone |
| 1885 Belgium acquires Congo | 1872–1928 Roald Amundsen, Norwegian explorer | 1876 Bell invents telephone |
| 1886 Germany and Britain divide East Africa | 1874–1965 Winston Churchill, British statesman | 1884 Waterman's fountain pen |
| 1899–1902 Anglo–Boer War | 1879–1953 Josef Stalin, Russian revolutionary | 1886–7 Benz and Daimler invent internal combustion engine |
| 1910 Union of South Africa formed | 1879–1955 Albert Einstein, German physicist | 1895 Marconi's radio |
| 1911 Italians conquer Libya | 1881–1938 Atatürk, Turkish statesman | 1903 First successful flight by Wright brothers |
| 1914 British Protectorate in Egypt | 1881–1973 Pablo Picasso, Spanish painter | 1909 Peary reaches North Pole |
| 1919 Nationalist revolt in Egypt | 1882–1945 Franklin Roosevelt, American statesman | 1911 Amundsen reaches South Pole |
| 1922 Egypt becomes independent | 1883–1945 Mussolini, Italian dictator | 1913 Geiger counter invented |
| 1936 Italy annexes Ethiopia | 1887–1978 Chiang Kai-shek, Chinese statesman | 1918 Automatic rifle invented |
| | 1889–1945 Adolf Hitler, German Nazi leader | 1919 Rutherford splits atom |
| | 1889–1964 Nehru, Indian leader | 1919 First crossing of Atlantic by air |
| 1949 Apartheid established in South Africa | 1889–1978 Jomo Kenyatta, Kenyan statesman | 1925 Baird invents television |
| 1956 Suez crisis | 1890–1970 General de Gaulle, French statesman | 1926 First liquid fuel rocket |
| 1957 Ghana becomes independent, followed by other African states | 1892–1975 Franco, Spanish dictator | 1930 Whittle's jet engine |
| | 1892–1980 Josip Tito, Yugoslavian statesman | The planet Pluto discovered |
| 1960 Civil war follows independence in the Congo | 1893–1976 Mao Zedong (Mao Tse-tung), Chinese revolutionary | 1935 Invention of nylon |
| 1967–70 Nigerian civil war | 1894–1971 Khrushchev, Soviet statesman | 1939 Development of penicillin |
| | 1909–1972 Kwame Nkrumah, Gold Coast nationalist | 1947 First supersonic flight |
| | 1898–1978 Golda Meir, Israeli stateswoman | 1948 Transistor developed |
| | 1913– Willi Brandt, German statesman | 1953 The conquest of Everest |
| 1979 General Amin flees from Uganda | 1914– Thor Heyerdahl, explorer | 1957 First satellite (U.S.S.R.) launched |
| 1980 Last British colony in Africa achieves independence as Zimbabwe | 1917–63 John F. Kennedy, American statesman | 1961 First man in space |
| 1981 President Sadat of Egypt assassinated | 1917–1984 Indira Gandhi, Indian stateswoman | 1969 Neil Armstrong first man on Moon |
| 1985 Renewed unrest in South Africa | 1918–1970 Gamal Nasser, Egyptian statesman | 1976 Microcomputers on a single chip |
| 1986 Ethiopia has worst famine in more than 10 years | 1924– Kenneth Kaunda, Zambian leader | 1981 First reusable Space Shuttle launched |
| | 1925– Margaret Thatcher, British prime minister | 1982 First successful, permanent artificial heart operation |
| | 1927– Fidel Castro, Cuban leader | 1986 Six new moons discovered around the planet Uranus |
| | 1929–68 Martin Luther King, Black American civil rights leader | 1987 World's longest surviving heart transplant patient dies |
| | 1934–68 Yuri Gagarin, first man in space | |

# Glossary

**Acropolis** The highest point of an Ancient Greek city. It was a citadel with strong defensive walls, and a sacred enclosure containing the chief temples of the city.

**Ally (Alliance)** A partner (partners) in peace or war.

**Amphitheater** An open air theater with rising tiers of seats arranged around a central stage.

**Annex** To take possession of land or a country, usually without having any rights to it.

**Assassinate** To murder someone, especially a political or religious leader, for political purposes.

**Barbarians** People living outside the borders of a developed society with a strong culture and way of life were often regarded by those inside as barbarians.

**Boers** Dutch colonists in South Africa, and their descendants.

**Bronze** An alloy (mixture) of copper and tin. It is much harder than pure copper and was first discovered about 3000 B.C.

**Caravan** A group of merchants or pilgrims traveling together, usually for safety.

**City-state** A city which ruled itself and the farmland around it.

**Civil war** War between groups of citizens of the same country.

**Colonize** To found settlements abroad which are ruled on behalf of the home country.

**Colony** A group of people living in a new country, but keeping ties with their home country.

**Communists** Members of a political party which believes that all property and means of production should belong to the State.

**Conquistador** The Spanish word for "conqueror." It is the name given to the Spanish adventurers who went to South America in search of treasure.

**Democracy** From Greek words meaning rule by the people. Usually, this means that a government is elected for fixed periods by the citizens of a State.

**Dynasty** A series of rulers from the same family.

**Emigrate** To leave the country of which you are a citizen to settle in another country.

**Empire** A group of countries under one ruler.

**Excavation** The unearthing of a historic site.

**Expedition** A journey taken for a special purpose.

**Fascism** The political theory that believes that the rights of individuals should take second place to the interests of the State.

**Feudalism** A system where a great lord or ruler owns the land, which he grants to lesser lords or peasants in return for services, usually military or work on the land.

**Guerilla** A member of an irregular military force which is usually split into small independent groups.

**Horde** A large tribe or troop of nomadic warriors.

**Imperialism** The rule of one people by another and the belief that a strong nation has a right and a duty to govern weaker nations.

**Medieval** The word used to describe something which is connected with the Middle Ages.

**Missionaries** People sent to make new converts to a religion, particularly in other countries.

**Mosaic** A picture or design produced by piecing together tiny pieces of glass and stone.

**Nomads** People who move with their flocks and herds in search of grazing land. Many nomads move only between summer and winter pastures.

**Pioneer** A person who goes to a new place or country to settle. It also means a person who is the first to do something.

**Plague** A disease which spreads rapidly killing large numbers of people.

**Plantation** A large estate growing one type of plant, looked after by workers living on the land under the direction of the owner.

**Refugees** Someone who is forced to leave their home by enemy or political action or by a natural disaster, and seek safety elsewhere.

**Spice Islands** The name given to the islands of Southeast Asia from which spices were exported to Europe. Today these islands are called the Moluccas in Indonesia.

**Steppes** The high, cold plains of Russia and central Asia.

**Terracotta** Clay which has been shaped and baked. It is often painted and glazed for decoration and to make it waterproof.

**Treaty** A written and signed agreement between countries relating to an alliance, trade etc.

**Tsar** The Russian form of the word "caesar," used for the ruler.

**Warsaw Pact** An alliance set up after World War II between the USSR and most of the countries of Eastern Europe.

# Index

Numbers in *italics* refer to illustrations or maps

**PHOTOGRAPHIC ACKNOWLEDGMENTS**

**Cover** *left to right* ZEFA, Robert Harding, ZEFA, ZEFA.
**Endpapers** Michael Holford; **page 7** *top* Sonia Halliday, *bottom* ZEFA; 10 Michael Holford; 12 *center* British Museum; 13 *top* ZEFA; 14 *top* British Museum, *center* Brooklyn Museum, *bottom* British Museum; 16 *top* Ronald Sheridan, *bottom* Sonia Halliday; 18 *left & right* ZEFA; 19 SCALA; 20 *top* ZEFA, *bottom* ZEFA; 22 *bottom* Sonia Halliday; 23 British Museum; 24 *left & right* Ronald Sheridan; 26 *left* Italian Ministry of Defence, *right* Michael Holford; 30 *center* Walters Art Gallery, Baltimore, *bottom left & right* Universitets Oldsaksamling, Oslo; 32 *center* Sonia Halliday, *bottom left* SCALA, *bottom right* British Museum; 34 Sonia Halliday; 35 Bibliothèque Nationale; 36 Giraudon, Paris; 39 Alan Hutchison; 40 *top & center* British Museum, *bottom* Mansell Collection; 42 *top* British Museum, *bottom* J. Allan Cash, 43 British Museum; 47 Michael Holford; 48 *center* British Museum, *bottom* Cooper-Bridgeman Library; 50 Bridgeman Art Library; 54 *center* ZEFA, *bottom* National Army Museum; 60 Mansell Collection; 61 National Portrait Gallery; 62 Peter Newark; 63 *center & bottom left* Mansell Collection, *bottom right* Mary Evans Picture Library; 66 Kyoto Costume Institute; 70 *top* Peter Clayton, *bottom left* Mary Evans Picture Library, *bottom right* Syndication International; 74 Alan Hutchison; 76 *left* Vision International/Paola Koch, *right* Frank Spooner Pictures; 78 *left* Alan Hutchison, *right* ZEFA.

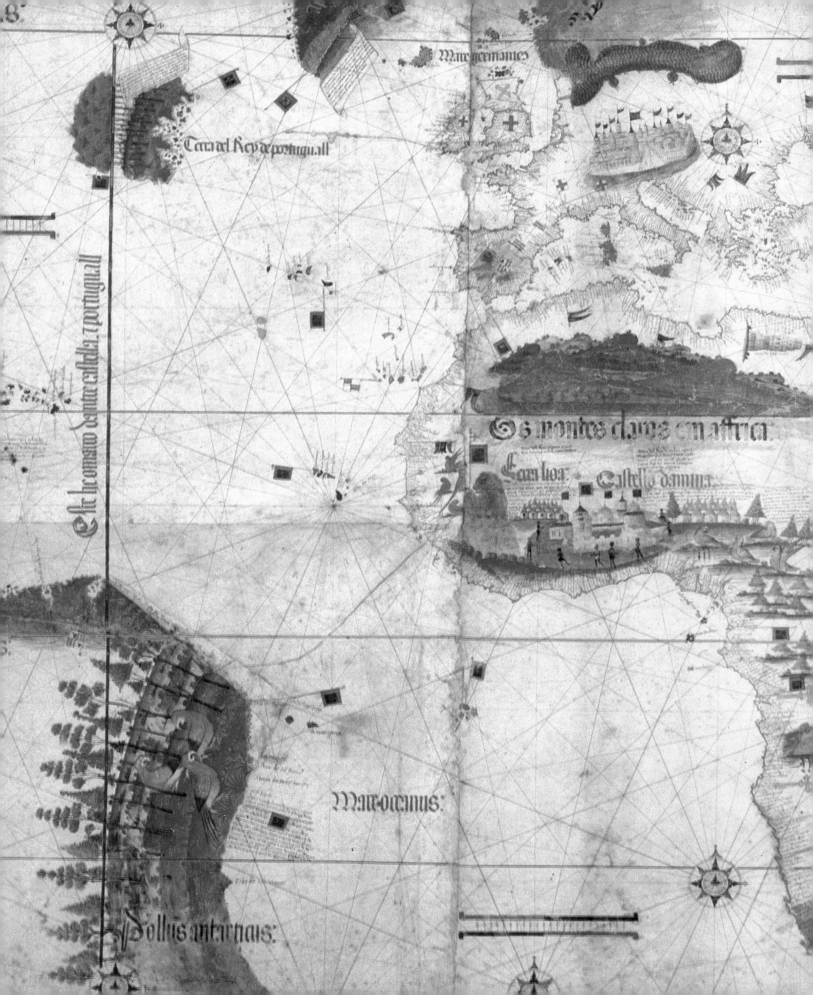

Mare germanus

Terra del Rey de portuguall

Elte lico maço dtra caftela. 7 portugall

Os montes claros em affrica.

Caualioa    Castello damina.

Marocenus:

Sollus antarnais: